ON FIRE!

HOLIDAY CLUB RESOURCE MATERIAL

ANGELA FLYNN & SUSAN CURRIE

A COMPLETE
FIVE-DAY HOLIDAY CLUB PROGRAMME
FOR 5s–11s+

GOD CENTRED AND BIBLE BASED

Leaders' notes for preparation, teaching and activities
Serial drama script
Craft ideas
Activity sheets
All-age family service or event

Scripture Union
130 City Road, London EC1V 2NJ

Publicity material designed especially for this programme is
available from Christian Publicity Organisation, Garcia Estate,
Canterbury Road, Worthing, W Sussex, BN13 1BW.

Copyright © Angela Flynn and Susan Currie 1994
First published 1994

British Library Cataloguing in Publication Data
A catalogue record for this book is available from
the British Library.

ISBN 0 86201887 0

The artwork, activity sheets and music in this book may be
photocopied for use in running the On Fire! holiday club
programme, without reference to current copyright legislation
or any copyright licensing scheme.

All rights reserved. No part of this publication may be
reproduced, stored in a retrieval system or transmitted, in any
form or by any means, electronic, mechanical, photocopying,
recording or otherwise, without the prior permission of
Scripture Union, except as indicated above. The right of
Angela Flynn and Susan Currie to be identified as authors of
this work has been asserted by them in accordance with the
Copyright, Designs and Patents Act 1988.

All Scripture quotations are taken from the Good News Bible
Old Testament: copyright © American Bible Society 1976;
New Testament: copyright © American Bible Society 1966,
1971, 1976.

Cover by Tony Cantale Graphics
Design and illustration by Tony Cantale Graphics

Printed in England by Ebenezer Baylis & Son Ltd,
The Trinity Press, Worcester and London

Contents

INTRODUCTION 5
    Countdown to On Fire! with suggested timetable 5
    The set 6
    The people 7
    The programme 8
    Daily essentials checklists 9
    On Fire! items to prepare 10
    On Fire! song 21–23

Day 1   **ALIGHT!** 24

Day 2   **BAG OF BONES** 29

Day 3   **THE RIDDLE** 34

Day 4   **ESCAPE!** 39

Day 5   **BLINDED** 44

Sofa Talk interview scripts 49

ALL-AGE FAMILY SERVICE OR EVENT 53

Activity sheets for 7s–9s   27, 32, 37, 42, 47
Activity sheets for 10s–11s   28, 33, 38, 43, 48
Research Notes for 10s–11s   54
Craft activity material   57

ADDITIONAL MATERIALS
available for use with this holiday club programme

**Scripture Union video
ON FIRE! THE VIDEO**
6 episodes featuring Roy Castle.
£14.99.

ON FIRE–EXTRA!
For the first time Scripture Union has produced a fun activity booklet for children to take home as a follow-on from the holiday club. Only 35p each in packs of 10.

Available from
your local Christian bookshop
or from
Scripture Union Mail Order,
9-11 Clothier Road,
Bristol BS4 5RL.
Tel. 0272 719709.

Introduction

On Fire! is a five-day holiday club programme for children aged five to eleven plus. It runs for one hour fifty minutes on five consecutive mornings during school holidays or half-terms. It is suitable both for children who have little or no Bible knowledge, and for children who have Christian adults at home. Through the lively, magazine-style programme with music, video, games, Bible teaching, crafts and drama we discover more about the Holy Spirit and how he can affect our lives. There are thoughtful, quieter moments too, for the children to think about their own response to the day's theme and activities.

There are a number of small group activities which help to develop one to one relationships between leaders and children as they talk, play games and make things together.

Approximate timings are given throughout the programme to help with your planning and to keep the programme moving.

COUNTDOWN TO ON FIRE!

It is best to begin preparations for a holiday club about nine months before. This gives time for assembling team and materials (you may want to ask church members to start collecting some craft materials). It also gives time for prayer and time for planning finance and publicity. Christian Publicity Organisation produce special On Fire! invitations and posters to help with publicising your holiday club. For more information write to CPO, Garcia Estate, Canterbury Road, Worthing, W Sussex BN13 1BW.

Think carefully about the space and facilities you need. Under the 1989 Children Act, a five-day holiday club with under-eights present lasting under two hours does not have to be registered with the social services department of your local authority, but you are obliged to inform them of the event. In addition, check that:

✔ toilets and wash basins are easily reached by young children
✔ you have an adequate first aid kit handy and preferably a qualified first aider on the team
✔ pens, paints, glues etc are non-toxic
✔ squash is additive-free (particularly of tartrazine)
✔ electrical equipment is not left unattended for children to play with
✔ strangers cannot easily enter your hall or meeting place
✔ there is roughly one group leader to six children
✔ there is adequate heating
✔ stone or rough wooden flooring is covered with rugs or carpet squares if children are to sit on the floor.

There are suggested programmes for a family service or event after On Fire! on page 53. The latter would be helpful if parents of most children at the holiday club are not used to being in church. The sixth episode of the video should be used at this event. Children will take home invitations on Day 5.

Suggested timetables for a whole morning or evening club are shown below.

See each day's Programme at a Glance to see how On Fire! runs.

MORNING
9.00	Team arrives
9.15-10.00	Bible study, prayer and preparation
10.00-11.50	Programme runs
11.50-12.30	Children leave, clear up
12.30-1.30	Team lunch, evaluation, tomorrow's briefing
1.30-2.00	Prepare for next day

EVENING
5.30	Team arrives, study, pray
6.00-7.30	Programme runs
7.30-8.00	Children leave
8.00-9.00	Evaluation, briefing, prepare for next day.

■ THE SET

On Fire! is set in a television studio. The leaders are Managers and the children are Reporters (5s-9s) and Production Crew (10s-11s). The hall should have a stage or raised area and seating for the children for the all together times. There should be enough space (possibly around the sides) for each small group to meet in. The theme colours for the whole holiday club are red, orange, yellow and white. Make a very large flame motif backdrop for stage area. Write around the flame, 'When the Holy Spirit comes upon you, you will be filled with power (Acts 1:8).' Some activities will need this flame backdrop.

Additional decorations for the hall if you have the time and personnel: silhouette of TV cameras and microphones, 'wall' of cardboard TV screens, additional spotlights.

All items below are needed daily.

VIDEO MONITORS
A large TV screen or linked monitors to show the On Fire! video, or a TV frame.

TV
For News Broadcast. Made from an old box placed in front of the TV news presenter sat at a table.

'ON AIR' LIGHT
This is a red light used on the stage to signal all together times. It should be switched off again as a signal for the children to go into small groups. A bulb or torch in a box covered in red paper and black lettering would be ideal.

COMFY SOFA
A large Chesterfield-type sofa or armchairs for 'Sofa Talk'. Sofa could be covered with a bedspread or blanket in the On Fire! colours.

'OVER TO YOU' HAND
This is a cardboard hand with pointing index finger attached to a broom handle. This is used at all points in the programme prior to the children being involved. Pick up the hand, point at the children and shout 'One, two' (team and children join in with) 'Over to you!'

COMMENTARY BOX

A post box is placed prominently so that the children can write to Managers, Presenters or other Reporters or Production Crew with questions or comments (see box on page 10).

BILLBOARD

Each day's headline summarising the day's theme is written on a large sheet of paper and placed on the billboard in the entrance hall. A billboard could be obtained from a newsagent.

DAILY ESSENTIALS FOR THE SET

- The set (outlined above)
- Microphone(s)
- Stopwatch, gong, scoreboard and floor covering for Beat the Bong
- Words for On Fire! song and other songs
- Sofa Talk interview script (for prompting)
- Commentary Box
- Stand and Deliver Box
- Beat the Bong Box

■ THE PEOPLE

THE PRODUCERS

One or two people are needed to co-ordinate the overall running of On Fire! They should be people with no small group or upfront responsibility, but free to maintain oversight of the proceedings and respond to any problems.

THE PRESENTERS

- **BOSS** acts as anchorman/woman, leads the singing, keeps the programme to time and introduces people who take part.
- **CORRIE SCOTT** is a typical chat show hostess who interviews the Bible characters during 'Sofa Talk'. She believes she knows everything. Children should recognise her as an over-the-top, self-important bully. (Adjust the name if using a male presenter.) Corrie dresses in smart TV-presenter style.
- **TERRY AND SAM** are senior editor and junior reporter who are a bit of a comedy double-act. They introduce joke sessions and some messy games.

INTERVIEW CHARACTER

Each day a character from the Bible story is interviewed. The scripts for these appear on page 49. The scripts are meant to be used as a springboard for your creativity, although they can be used as they are.

Each biblical character makes an appearance in the entrance hall at the end of the day before their interview. This acts as a teaser or 'trailer' for the next day.

MANAGERS

These are the small group leaders. They should be dressed in plain 'On Fire!' colours. You may want to get special t-shirts produced with the logo.

REPORTERS AND PRODUCTION CREW

These are the children.

TECHNICAL DIRECTOR

This is an important role. He or she may be responsible for any microphones, amplifiers, projectors and stage lighting you decide to use and perhaps help the Production Crew with the camcorder. If the On Fire! video is being used, the Technical Director will need to link up a video cassette recorder to one or more TV monitors. (Please write to the Scripture Union Sound and Vision Unit, 130 City Road, London EC1V 2NJ for a useful sheet about this.) This need not be a 'high-tech' role, but if you use a lot of electrical equipment, check that sockets and wiring are safe and that long flexes are secured.

THE BAND

(Should include a guitarist.)
The band is responsible for the music. They may lead the singing, but it's ideal if Boss can do this. The On Fire! song is printed on page 22. Other songs suitable can be found in *Junior Praise 1 & 2*. It's probably best to stick to the same four or five songs throughout the week so that children can get to know them well. Suggested songs: Be bold, be strong; Father God I wonder; I'm special; When the Spirit of the Lord; If you climb; God loves you.

■ THE PROGRAMME

The programme contains the same elements each day which are represented by symbols so the running order can be seen at a glance. If you need to cut programme elements, make sure that you cut the same items each day. Headliners, Take Five, Beat the Bong and Stand and Deliver are suitable for cutting if you're short of time.

REGISTRATION

Children are registered as they arrive. You will need to record each day the children who come in case of fire or other emergency. The registration card is on page 14. If you have more than one church involved, you may wish to record the name of a friend with whom each child comes. You can then direct him or her to that church after the holiday club. Record any allergies, recurring illnesses etc on the reverse.

PRESS PASSES AND PRODUCTION CREW BADGES

These are shown on pages 16 and 17. Photocopy, cut out and stick onto thin card. Thread elastic through the hole in the top for the children to wear each day. Cards can be colour-coded for different age groups. Names and ages should be added at the first registration time. You could add a small photo of the child if you wished.

FAST FORWARD

This is the main Bible teaching input. The appropriate episode from the video On Fire! is shown. There are six stories; one for each day and one for the family service or event.

NEWS BROADCAST

This is the alternative to using the video. A scripted news bulletin is read each day, giving the Bible story. You will need to make a television shown on page 11. This is placed around the head of the team member giving the broadcast. The broadcasts last one or two minutes. Each episode of the video lasts seven minutes. This means you have an extra five minutes to use elsewhere in the programme.

SOFA TALK

This is a scripted interview between Corrie Scott and each Bible character. Sofa Talk aims to help the children identify with the characters. It takes place on a sofa or armchairs on the set.

TAKE 5

Five minute break for squash and biscuits.

KARAOKE PRAISE

Praise songs and general participation in worship activities. When the songs are familiar, Boss could wander among the children allowing some to sing into a microphone. This needs to be done sensitively as some children will be shy and it would be inappropriate during quiet, prayerful songs.

POWER PACK

Craft activities to be done in the small groups. There are extra craft ideas included later in the programme.

HEADLINERS

This is the opening activity which helps children to get involved as soon as they arrive. Managers help their Reporters or Production Crew members. Make five or six headshapes a metre in diameter before the holiday club. Add hair and features (see page 11). The mouth is left blank to hold each day's activity information (photos, magazine cut-outs). The headliner heads are left as part of the set.

STAND AND DELIVER

This is joke time. Each day different sorts of jokes are told by the children and by Sam and Terry. Children are asked to write out jokes with their names and put them in the Stand and Deliver Box (see page 10).

BEAT THE BONG

This is a challenge game which involves a small number of children and takes place up-front. Most games are messy so the children must be volunteers. Names go in the Beat the Bong Box (see box on page 10).

OFFICE TIME

This is small group time. There should be a maximum of eight children to a group with two adult team members. To allow relationships and trust to be built up, the children stay in the same groups all week. Chat to the children informally about On Fire! and about the things they are learning. On the first day of the holiday club, all children make a clipboard on which they keep all their activity sheets and stickers as a record of the holiday club. At the end of Office Time each day, everyone is given an 'I've Covered It' sticker for their clipboard. These can be photocopied from page 18 and cut out in advance. Stick on the clipboards with stick adhesive. Children can take the clipboards home after Day 5.

DAILY ESSENTIALS FOR OFFICE TIME

- Paper or forms for entries in the various boxes.
- Headliner quiz sheets
- Pencils and rubbers
- Felt tip pens
- Clipboards
- 'I've Covered It!' stickers for each day
- Activity sheets for relevant age group
- Good News Bibles for Production Crew research
- Managers' own lists of names of children in their groups.

Each Manager could have a tray or cardboard box labelled with office name to keep materials in.

ON FIRE! SONG

The theme song for the holiday club. Words, music and actions on pages 21-23.

OVER TO YOU!

Your cue to pick up the large hand, point at the children and use the slogan, 'One, two' (children shout back) 'over to you!'

ON AIR

This signals an all together time in the programme. Switch on for this time.

■ **THE 5s-6s (REPORTERS)** make a television set out of shoe boxes. Each day they have an activity sheet to colour in showing the Bible story. These are put together to make a short filmstrip which they can wind through their television.

■ **THE 7s-9s (REPORTERS)** use the daily Newsflash sheets to compile a newspaper about the Bible stories through the week.

■ **THE 10s-11s (PRODUCTION CREW)** make a documentary-style video about the holiday club, 'The On Fire Experience'. Each day the Research notes help them think through the Bible story. The Production Crew Assignment sheets help them plan the video and decide what will be shot. You will need to obtain a camcorder for the fourth day of the holiday club when the Production Crew will shoot the video. Invite someone who knows how to use the camcorder to brief the Production Crew managers before the holiday club and to give technical back-up to the Production Crew and managers during the week.

If you anticipate fifteen or more 10s-12s, consider dividing into two groups working with two cameras.

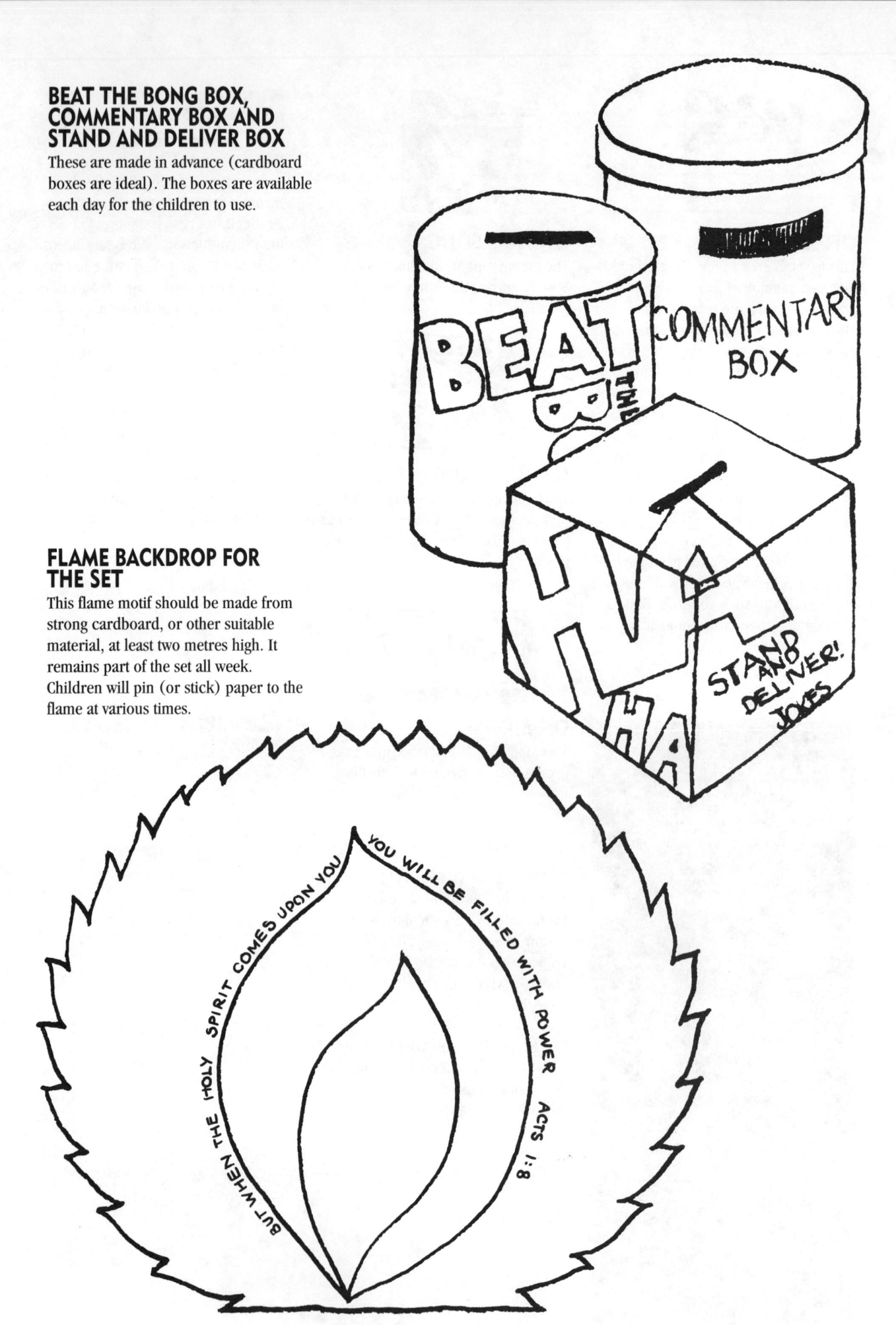

BEAT THE BONG BOX, COMMENTARY BOX AND STAND AND DELIVER BOX

These are made in advance (cardboard boxes are ideal). The boxes are available each day for the children to use.

FLAME BACKDROP FOR THE SET

This flame motif should be made from strong cardboard, or other suitable material, at least two metres high. It remains part of the set all week. Children will pin (or stick) paper to the flame at various times.

THE 'TV' BOX FOR NEWS BROADCAST

A strong cardboard box cut to resemble a TV set is ideal. It is 'worn' by the newscaster.

HEADSHAPES HEAD

You will need to make five or six large round headshapes with large mouth for Headliner activity each day.

OVER TO YOU! HAND

Large hand with pointing finger attached to broom handle. Make from cardboard or balsa wood

BILLBOARD

'ON AIR' LIGHT

12

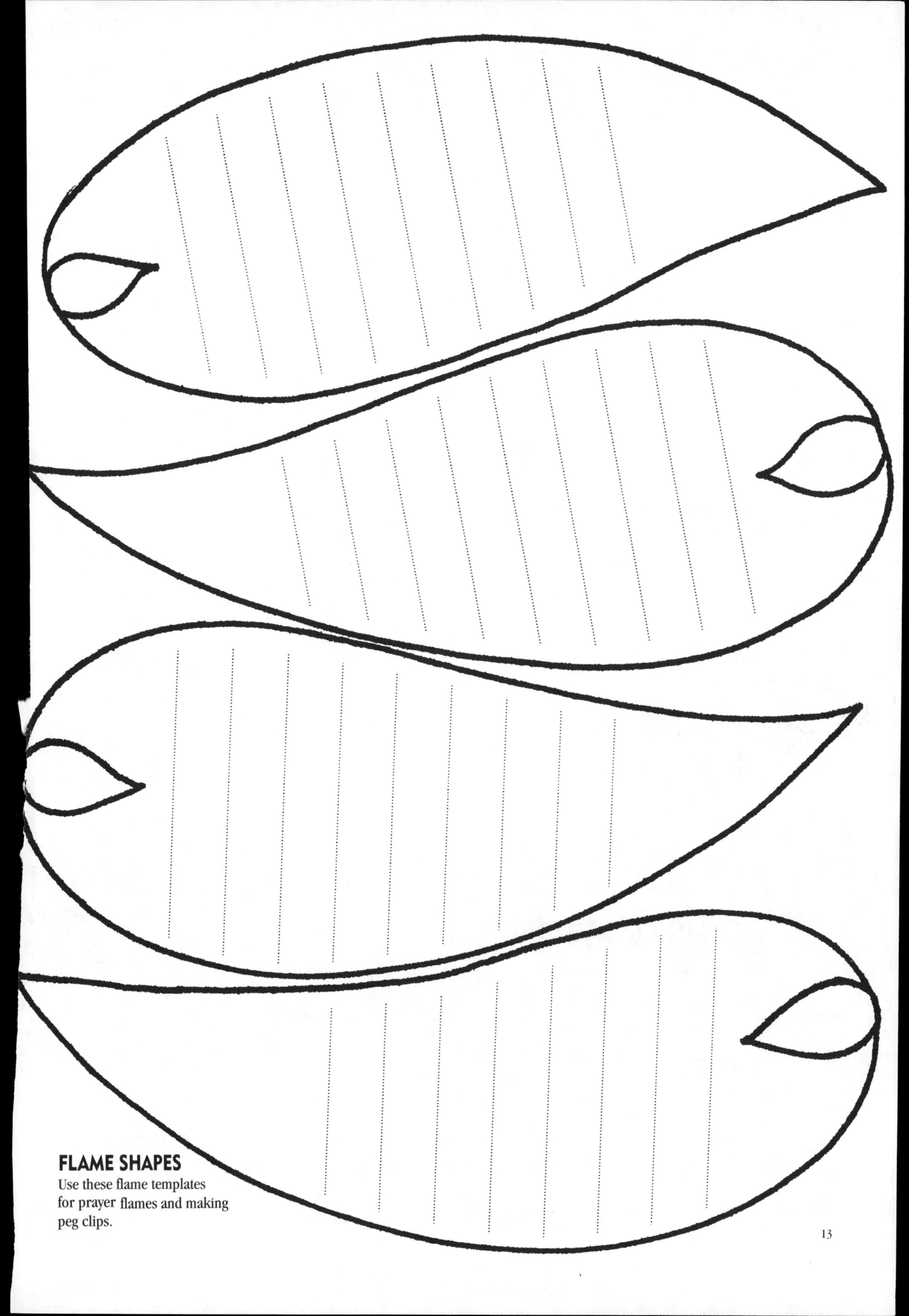

FLAME SHAPES
Use these flame templates for prayer flames and making peg clips.

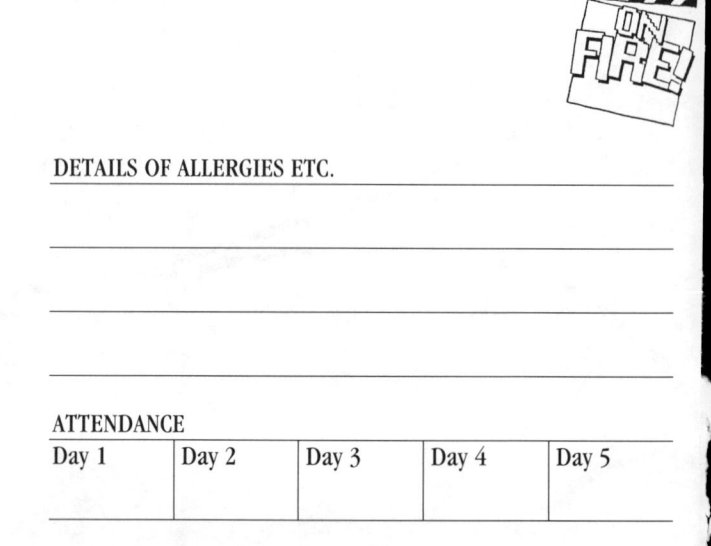

REGISTRATION CARD

SURNAME

FIRST NAME   AGE

ADDRESS

PARENT/GUARDIAN

Where they can be contacted

DETAILS OF ALLERGIES ETC.

ATTENDANCE

Day 1	Day 2	Day 3	Day 4	Day 5

NEWS OFFICE TEAM

REGISTRATION CARD

SURNAME

FIRST NAME   AGE

ADDRESS

PARENT/GUARDIAN

Where they can be contacted

DETAILS OF ALLERGIES ETC.

ATTENDANCE

Day 1	Day 2	Day 3	Day 4	Day 5

NEWS OFFICE TEAM

REGISTRATION CARD

SURNAME

FIRST NAME   AGE

ADDRESS

PARENT/GUARDIAN

Where they can be contacted

DETAILS OF ALLERGIES ETC.

ATTENDANCE

Day 1	Day 2	Day 3	Day 4	Day 5

NEWS OFFICE TEAM

REGISTRATION CARD

SURNAME _____

FIRST NAME _____ AGE _____

ADDRESS _____

_____

_____

PARENT/GUARDIAN _____

Where they can be contacted _____

_____

DETAILS OF ALLERGIES ETC. _____

_____

_____

_____

ATTENDANCE

Day 1	Day 2	Day 3	Day 4	Day 5

NEWS OFFICE TEAM

_____

REGISTRATION CARD

SURNAME _____

FIRST NAME _____ AGE _____

ADDRESS _____

_____

_____

PARENT/GUARDIAN _____

Where they can be contacted _____

_____

DETAILS OF ALLERGIES ETC. _____

_____

_____

_____

ATTENDANCE

Day 1	Day 2	Day 3	Day 4	Day 5

NEWS OFFICE TEAM

_____

REGISTRATION CARD

SURNAME _____

FIRST NAME _____ AGE _____

ADDRESS _____

_____

_____

PARENT/GUARDIAN _____

Where they can be contacted _____

_____

DETAILS OF ALLERGIES ETC. _____

_____

_____

_____

ATTENDANCE

Day 1	Day 2	Day 3	Day 4	Day 5

NEWS OFFICE TEAM

_____

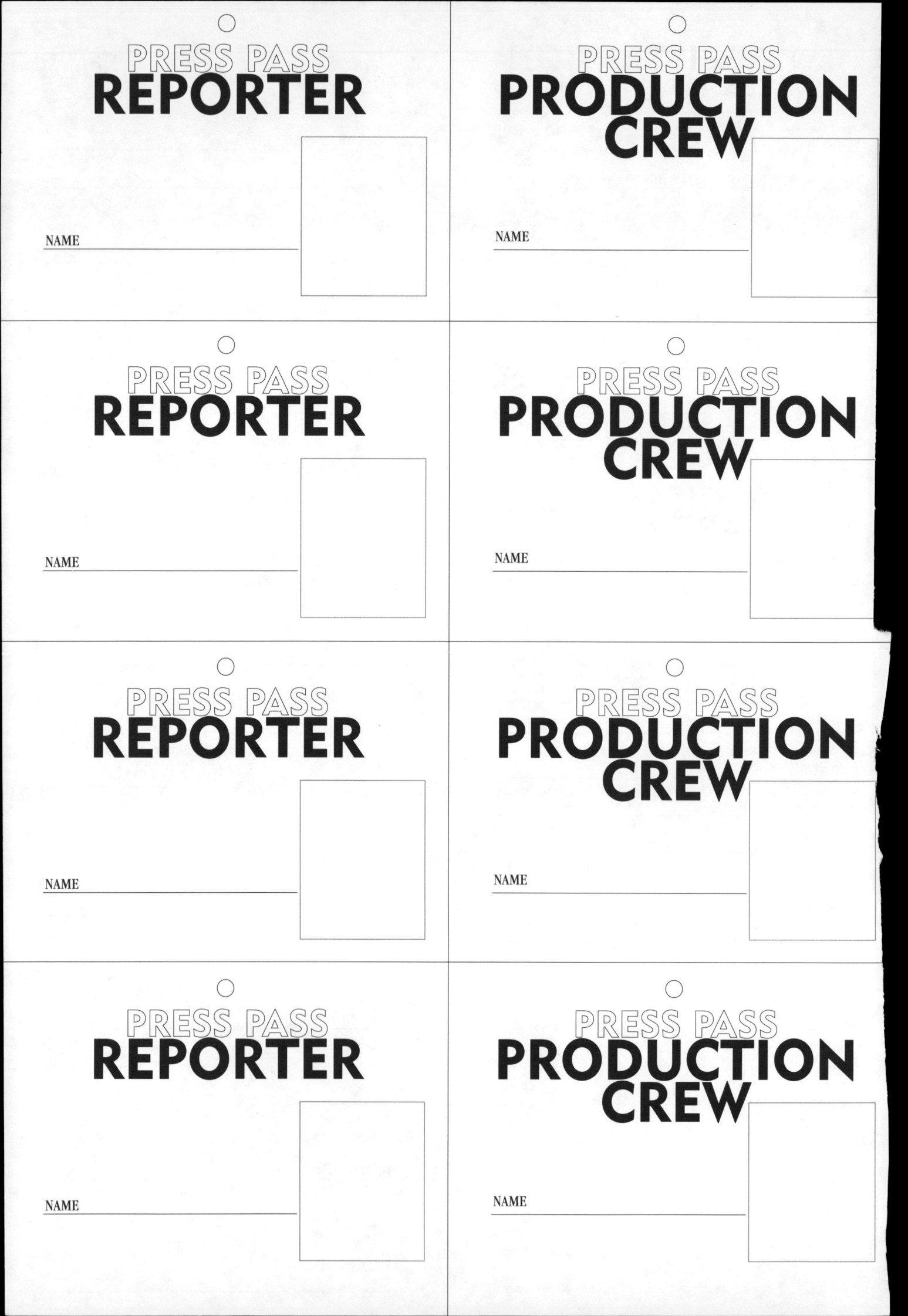

PRESS PASS
REPORTER
NAME

PRESS PASS
PRODUCTION CREW
NAME

PRESS PASS
REPORTER
NAME

PRESS PASS
PRODUCTION CREW
NAME

PRESS PASS
REPORTER
NAME

PRESS PASS
PRODUCTION CREW
NAME

PRESS PASS
REPORTER
NAME

PRESS PASS
PRODUCTION CREW
NAME

PRESS PASS	PRESS PASS
REPORTER	**PRODUCTION CREW**
NAME	NAME

PRESS PASS	PRESS PASS
REPORTER	**PRODUCTION CREW**
NAME	NAME

PRESS PASS	PRESS PASS
REPORTER	**PRODUCTION CREW**
NAME	NAME

PRESS PASS	PRESS PASS
REPORTER	**PRODUCTION CREW**
NAME	NAME

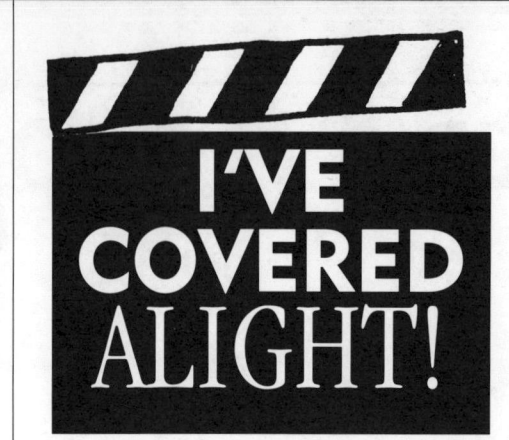

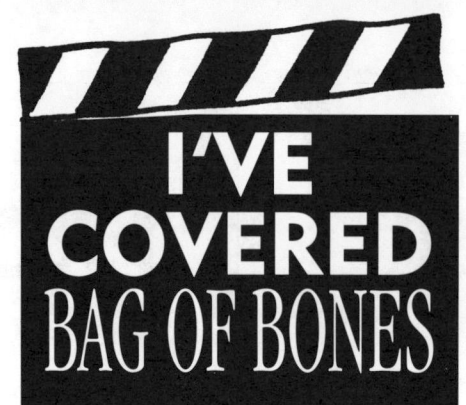

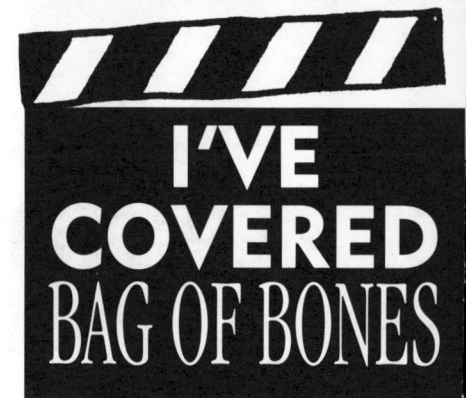

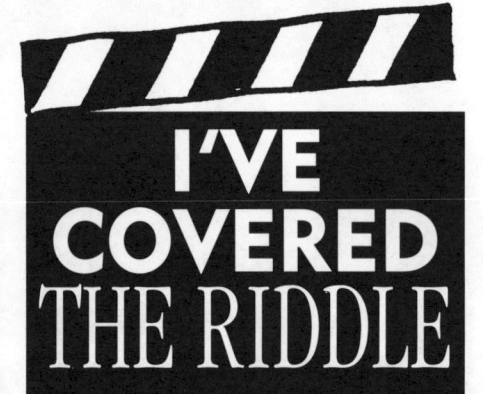

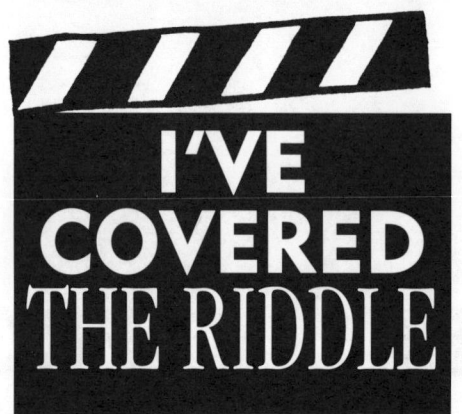

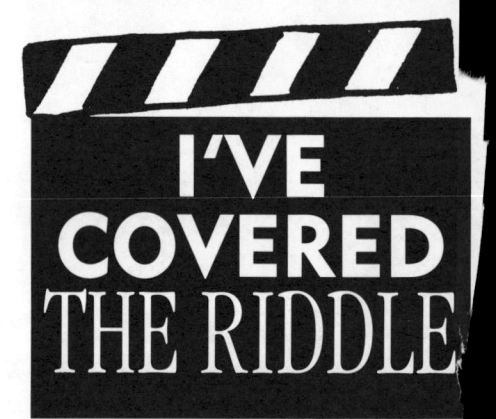

I'VE COVERED ALIGHT!	**I'VE COVERED ALIGHT!**	**I'VE COVERED ALIGHT!**
I'VE COVERED BAG OF BONES	**I'VE COVERED BAG OF BONES**	**I'VE COVERED BAG OF BONES**
I'VE COVERED THE RIDDLE	**I'VE COVERED THE RIDDLE**	**I'VE COVERED THE RIDDLE**
I'VE COVERED ESCAPE!	**I'VE COVERED ESCAPE!**	**I'VE COVERED ESCAPE!**
I'VE COVERED BLINDED!	**I'VE COVERED BLINDED!**	**I'VE COVERED BLINDED!**

STAND AND DELIVER

MY JOKE IS

_____
_____
_____
_____
_____
_____
_____
_____

MY NAME IS
_____

STAND AND DELIVER

MY JOKE IS

_____
_____
_____
_____
_____
_____
_____
_____

MY NAME IS
_____

BEAT THE BONG VOLUNTEER

I WANT TO VOLUNTEER

NAME
_____

NEWS OFFICE TEAM
_____

BEAT THE BONG VOLUNTEER

I WANT TO VOLUNTEER

NAME
_____

NEWS OFFICE TEAM
_____

HEADLINER
QUIZ SHEET

HEADLINER
QUIZ SHEET

COMMENTARY BOX
SHEET

DEAR

COMMENTARY BOX
SHEET

DEAR

The On Fire! song

Words and music by Angela Flynn

WORDS

I gotta warm feeling in my bones,
Tingling from my head down to my toes,
Inside I'm starting to glow.
I think I'm on fire!

It begins when I start to pray,
Glows when I hear your name,
Heats up when I sing your praise.
I think I'm on fire!

On fire with God's love,
On fire with his praise,
On fire with his power.
On fire today.

On fire with your love,
On fire with your praise,
On fire with your power.
Help me to stay
On fire every day.

On fire ... x 7

ACTIONS

VERSE 1

I GOTTA WARM FEELING IN MY BONES,
Bend arms at chest height, elbows sticking out horizontally. Spread fingers apart and wiggle in time to music.

TINGLING FROM MY HEAD DOWN TO MY TOES,
Move hands up to head, and still wiggling fingers move down to toes.

INSIDE I'M STARTING TO GLOW.
Move wiggling fingers from toes back to starting position on chest.

I THINK I'M ON FIRE!
Move wiggling fingers from chest to outstretched arms either side of chest.

VERSE 2

IT BEGINS WHEN I START TO PRAY,
Move hands to 'praying' position but keep them slightly apart, fingers wiggling.

GLOWS WHEN I HEAR YOUR NAME,
Move wiggling fingers to either side of head, near ears.

HEATS UP WHEN I SING YOUR PRAISE.
Arms straight above head wiggling fingers.

I THINK I'M ON FIRE!
Move wiggling fingers from chest to outstretched arms either side of chest.

As song gets louder the actions become more exaggerated. The next section of the song is an opportunity for everyone to make up their own actions – perhaps in reporters/production groups etc. Until that confidence comes, just clap!

The On Fire! song

Words and music by Angela Flynn

I gotta warm feeling in my bones, Tingling from my head down to my toes, In side I'm starting to glow. I think I'm on fire! It be gins when I start to pray, Glows when I hear your name, Heats up when I sing your praise. I think I'm on fire!

On fire with God's love, On fire with his praise, On fire with his power. On fire to day. On fire with your love, On fire with your praise, On fire with your power. Help me to stay On fire every day.

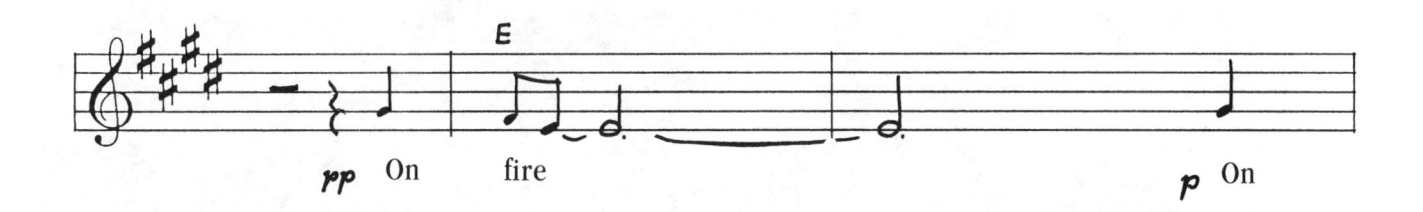

I gotta warm feeling in my bones,
Tingling from my head down to my toes,
Inside I'm starting to glow.
I think I'm on fire!

It begins when I start to pray,
Glows when I hear your name,
Heats up when I sing your praise.
I think I'm on fire!

On fire with God's love,
On fire with his praise,
On fire with his power.
On fire today.

On fire with your love,
On fire with your praise,
On fire with your power.
Help me to stay
On fire every day.

On fire ... x 7

Day 1
ALIGHT!

BIBLE MATERIAL: ACTS 2:1-41
INTERVIEW CHARACTER: PETER

TODAY'S OBJECTIVES
- To find out how the Holy Spirit empowered Peter and the other disciples at the first Pentecost.
- To explore how the Holy Spirit can do the same for us.

TEAM CHALLENGE

◆**THINK.** Jerusalem was packed with people who had come to celebrate Pentecost. This was a joyful occasion, a harvest festival, which took place fifty days after Passover. The Jews were encouraged to worship at the Temple for this festival and would travel from far and wide to Jerusalem. They were also encouraged to share this festival with foreigners (Lev 23:15-22, Deut 16:9-11) which gave a cosmopolitan flavour to the celebrations.

As Jews, the disciples would have been part of this joyful feast. However, they were also waiting for the fulfilment of Jesus' promise that he would send the Holy Spirit. He had explained about the work of the Holy Spirit to them (John 14:15-27,16:5-16) so they knew what to expect. What they weren't aware of was how and when the Holy Spirit would come. The description of what happened is dramatic indeed.

The sound of strong winds and tongues of fire were followed by the ability to speak in other languages. Peter preached, and 3,000 people became followers of Jesus.

◆**READ** Acts 2:1-41. The disciples had spent three years with Jesus. They had witnessed miracles, listened to his teachings, seen him die and rise again and been promised a secure future with him (John 14:2-4). However, without his physical presence with them they needed the Holy Spirit.

◆**CONSIDER** Peter, the demoralised coward who had denied Jesus; the man who was forgiven and accepted again by him, and now, by the Holy Spirit's power, the authoritative preacher. What a difference the Holy Spirit made to him! As we think about our On Fire! theme today, reflect on the fires in Peter's experience. He denied Jesus standing by a charcoal fire; he received Jesus' forgiveness and acceptance whilst breakfast was cooking on an open fire; finally he received the Holy Spirit in tongues of fire which transformed his life.

◆**PRAY** that the Holy Spirit's fire might come and burn away the useless and sinful things that could spoil your ministry today.

The disciples needed the Holy Spirit's power to preach the good news and we do too. Are we so familiar with running holiday clubs that we no longer rely on God for supernatural power? Or do we simply not see the need for something special this week? God longs to give us the Holy Spirit especially for the ministry he's called us to this week. We often don't realise how much we need empowering until we actually experience it, then wonder whatever we did without it!

◆**PRAY** together for the Holy Spirit to come in power to the whole team today and equip you for the task of being 'good news' this week.

■ YOU WILL NEED

HEADLINERS
- Photographs of the leaders as babies and as they are now.
- Headliner quiz sheets.

POWER PACKS
- All groups make clipboards (see page 61)
- Selection of craft material for collage
- Pre-cut paper flame shapes
- Cut-outs from magazines
- Photocopies of On Fire! logos
- A4 size card (backing from file paper pads or cereal boxes)
- Bulldog clips
- White stickers to write children's names on.

BEAT THE BONG: 'CHANGE YOUR LOOKS'
- Two pots of white face cream
- Two bright red lipsticks
- Two containers of dark eye shadow
- Two tubs of face powder or talc and cotton wool
- Two blushers with brushes
- Two wigs
- Two old shirts or towels
- Two straight backed chairs

- Two neck ties
- Scoreboard (large sheet of paper and pen or blackboard and chalk)

DON'T FORGET
- Good news/bad news jokes
- Shaving foam
- Paper plate
- Hand towel.
- Billboard headline PETER AND FRIENDS GIVEN POWER. Write in bold black print on flip chart paper with the On Fire! logo.
- Tomorrow's headline LAME MAN JUMPS FOR JOY!, should be ready for the end of today.
- Two remote-control cars, one larger than the other.
- Batteries for the smaller car only.
- Pre-cut paper flame shapes in the On Fire! colours.
- Pencils
- 'I've covered it!' stickers
- Peter in costume
- Lame man in costume with crutch for appearance at the close of today's programme.

PROGRAMME AT A GLANCE

	min
Registration and Headliners	15
Welcome and On Fire! song	10
Power Packs	20
Stand and Deliver	5
Car Race	5
Fast Forward	10
Sofa Talk	5
Take 5	5
Office Time	15
Beat the Bong	10
Karaoke Praise	10

PROGRAMME

REGISTRATION

HEADLINERS
Managers hand out Headliner quiz sheets and pencils. Place photographs of some of the leaders as babies in numbered headshapes round the room. Give each child a sheet with three leaders' names to choose from for each of the photographs. In order to give the children some help, up-to-date photographs of the same leaders labelled with their names should be placed on a noticeboard. This should help the children to familiarise themselves with some of the leaders' names. The headshapes will be needed tomorrow so the photographs should only be fixed temporarily.

ON AIR

Play the On Fire! song tune as everyone assembles.

Boss welcomes everyone to the On Fire! studio. He introduces team members and introduces the children as Reporters or Production Crew. Encourage them to stand and bow amid clapping and cheering. He explains the Commentary Box, the 'Over to you!' hand (practise the slogan) to indicate when everyone goes to their groups. Boss and the music group teach everyone the On Fire! song and actions. Boss shows everyone his clipboard.

Enter Corrie Scott demanding that she conducts her important interview now. Boss placates her. Exit Corrie. Boss explains that Corrie is the famous TV presenter of 'Sofa Talk' - and she knows it! Corrie is bossy and generally difficult.

OVER TO YOU!
Pick up hand and use slogan.

OFF AIR

POWER PACKS
Reporters and Production Crew make their own clipboards. Decorate with paper flame shapes, cut-outs from magazines and On Fire! logos. Each board should be named and have a bulldog clip. Clipboards hold Headliner quiz sheets, Newsflash, Production Crew Research notes, Assignment sheets and anything the children wish to keep on them.

ON AIR

STAND AND DELIVER
Terry and Sam tell good news/bad news jokes today and are joined by other members of the team. This should involve a change of joke-tellers working in two's running on and off the stage.

The good news is: You've been invited to my birthday party.
The bad news is: It was yesterday!
The good news is: We've found the pair of glasses you lost.
The bad news is: Sam found them when he sat on them!
The good news is: I've just made an interesting discovery. I've found a creature with twenty legs, two horns and sharp teeth.
The bad news is: It's crawling up your back!
The good news is: I've made you a cake!
The bad news is: It's in your face! (Push 'custard pie' in the face!)

Invite children to hand in 'Doctor, doctor' jokes for use tomorrow. Jokes could be given to Managers or put in the Joke Box.

Corrie makes a brief entrance saying, 'I don't allow stupid jokes in my interviews - when I'm allowed to have them!' Corrie storms off. Terry and Sam pretend to be terrified of Corrie.

Boss announces a car race between the Senior News Correspondent (Sam) and the Junior Reporter (Terry). Sam boasts that he's going to win because his car is bigger and faster (the children don't know that the batteries are missing from Sam's car). Terry has the smaller car. Boss asks the Reporters and Production Crew who they think is going to win. If possible hold the race down the centre of the room so that the children can stand either side. When the race starts it becomes obvious that Terry is going to win because Sam's car doesn't start. Cheer and clap Terry. Sam complains to Boss that his car doesn't work. Boss examines it and shows everyone that the batteries are missing. What a disaster! No wonder it wouldn't work. Explain that Jesus promised his friends that they would receive special power while they were in Jerusalem. And he was as good as his word ...

FAST FORWARD
Episode 1 'Alight' from *On Fire! – The Video*
or
NEWS BROADCAST
(Newsreader sitting inside TV frame.)
❝Reports have reached us today of strange events in Jerusalem.

The city is crowded with people from many different countries who have gathered for the Pentecost celebrations. The followers of Jesus were meeting together, when suddenly the sound of a mighty wind rushed through the house. This was immediately followed by what were described as 'tongues of fire' coming to rest on the disciples' heads. It appears that this was something special they had been waiting for. Jesus, the man who was God's Son, had promised to send the Holy Spirit. This is exactly what happened! Jesus' friends (called 'disciples') appeared to have the amazing ability to speak in all the different languages spoken by the crowd. So everyone could understand what they were talking about!

Peter was the main speaker and he told the crowd about Jesus of Nazareth who was executed less than two months ago. However, there have been rumours that he is alive again!

This is what Peter said in his speech today. He spoke with such power that lots of people believed him and 3000 of them became friends of Jesus this very day!❞

SOFA TALK 1
Script on page 49.

OFF AIR

TAKE 5
Break for drink and biscuit.

OFFICE TIME
Each group of Reporters chooses a newspaper title - Bournemouth Daily, Newport News, Yeovil Times, Edinburgh Echo, Wakefield Herald, Londonderry Messenger.
- 5s-6s colour in their first film strip ready for their 'television' tomorrow.
- 7s-9s Use today's Newsflash sheet to be clipped onto the clipboards. At the end of the week the five sheets will be stapled together to make a newspaper.
- 10s-11s Production Crew use Research notes 1 and Assignment Sheet 1 to start work on their documentary video 'The On Fire! Experience'.

Use this time to chat informally to the children. 'How did the disciples feel when Jesus died?' 'What difference did the Holy Spirit make to them?' There is time to pray with the children and there are suggested prayers on Newsflash sheets.

Hand out 'I've covered it!' stickers for clipboards.

ON AIR

BEAT THE BONG
'Change your looks'. Managers and team members take part today but from tomorrow Reporters and Production Crew volunteer. Two leaders wearing overalls sit on straight-backed chairs with their arms tied behind their backs. Two more leaders kneel behind the seated pair and thread their arms through under the seated leaders' arms as if to replace them. The seated leaders have a tray of make-up and a wig on their laps and give verbal instructions to the kneeling partner as to where the various items on the tray are. Sound the gong after one minute. Children can vote for a winner.

Boss reminds the children that the change that took place in Peter was on the inside, not the outside!

KARAOKE PRAISE
Hand out paper flame shapes and pencils. Boss draws attention to the way the Holy Spirit came to the disciples and gave them power. He can help us too. We can ask God for the power of his Spirit to help those we love, or to help us with things we find difficult. The 'flames' remind us of the 'tongues of fire' that touched the disciples. Children write on the prayer flames the things with which they would like the Holy Spirit to help them. Younger children could draw the person or situation they want to pray about. Tell them not to worry about spelling or writing because God will understand their prayer.

Either ask the children to all shout out together their prayer requests on the count of three, or pray that God by the power of his Holy Spirit, will hear our prayers. Prayer flames are attached to the flame backdrop behind the set.

Sing the On Fire! song again.

Enter Terry with tomorrow's billboard, LAME MAN JUMPS FOR JOY! Close with

'The bad news is: We've got to go now.
The good news is: We're back tomorrow at ...'.

Children encouraged to put names in boxes to volunteer for Stand and Deliver or Beat the Bong tomorrow. Managers could help with writing out children's jokes.

OFF AIR

■ The 'lame man' is sitting silently by the door as the children go out.

Day 2
BAG OF BONES

BIBLE MATERIAL: ACTS 3:1-10
INTERVIEW CHARACTER: THE LAME MAN

TODAY'S OBJECTIVES
- To discover that the Holy Spirit worked through Peter and John to heal the lame man.
- To explore the ways in which God heals people today.

TEAM CHALLENGE
The early Christians were firmly rooted in the Jewish faith. They were regular worshippers at the Temple and fulfilled everything that was required of orthodox observers of the faith. On this occasion Peter and John were going to the mid-afternoon prayer meeting in the Temple. They entered by the Beautiful Gate which the Jewish historian Josephus records as being close to, or known as, Nicanor's Gate, and was encrusted with precious metals. What a contrast to the lame man who had sat there begging for most of his life. Peter and John had changed so much by the Holy Spirit's power that they knew that they could offer the man much more than money. With total confidence in God, Peter asked the man to stand up and walk. The evidence of his healing was overwhelming - he didn't just walk, he leapt in the air!

◆**READ** Acts 3:1-10 and reflect on the contrasts in the story. A lame man living in abject poverty, sitting by a place of worship, the entrance to which was covered in priceless, precious metals. It must have been embarrassing to walk by him to attend worship in the Temple. What would you do? Throw a few coins or ignore him? Faced with him Peter and John decided to offer what they had. It certainly wasn't money - they had none. But they did have confidence in God. The Holy Spirit gave power in Jesus' name.

◆**DISCUSS** What have we got to offer the children? Write down some ideas.

The lame man had known nothing except the monotonous boredom and humiliation of begging. He was living under severe restrictions. God brought such healing to his life that these restrictions were broken. Physically he could walk, emotionally he was filled with joy and spiritually he was released into praising God in the Temple.

◆**PRAISE** Spend some time praising God in prayer or song.

PROGRAMME AT A GLANCE
	min
Registration and Headliners	10
On Fire! song	3
Fast Forward	10
Office Time	20
Beat the Bong	15
Stand and Deliver	5
Take 5	5
Karaoke Praise	15
Power Packs	20
Sofa Talk	5

■ YOU WILL NEED:

HEADLINERS
- Pictures of sports personalities known to children (preferably involved in the sport for which they are famous).
- Answer list.
- 'I've covered it!' stickers

BEAT THE BONG: 'HOW DO YOU FEEL?'
- Three overalls or old shirts
- Covering for floor
- A clear plastic or glass tank
- Bucket of thick cold custard (brightly coloured, made with water)
- 10 small items of different shapes
- Blindfold
- Stopwatch and gong
- Scoreboard
- Kitchen roll and large kitchen spoon

POWER PACKS
(Have clipboard materials for children who arrive for the first time today.)
5-6s make a TV set (see page 61)
- One shoe box per child
- Small plastic caps from bottles/tubes
- Plain paper to cover boxes (each box needs to have slits cut in the front for the film strip to feed through)
- Scissors
- PVA adhesive
- Overalls or old shirts

7s-9s make a paper fastener man
(see page 61)
- Paper fasteners
- paper
- string (optional)

DON'T FORGET
- Childrens' 'doctor, doctor' jokes with their names
- Paper hand shapes
- Pencils
- Lame man in costume with crutch or walking stick.
- Philip in costume with a pair of glasses and a Bible for appearance at the end of the programme.
- Today's billboard LAME MAN JUMPS FOR JOY.
- Tomorrow's billboard for use later, PHILIP EXPLAINS IT ALL.

PROGRAMME

REGISTRATION

HEADLINERS
Managers welcome the children and return clipboards and badges. Hand out Headliner quiz sheets.

Pictures of sports personalities are placed in the headshapes round the room. Three alternative names given for each one. Children underline the correct name. Display answers.

ON AIR

Boss welcomes children.

He or she opens Commentary Box and reads out comments, distributes day's post.

ON FIRE! SONG
Read out the words of the song slowly to give the children time to consider the meaning. Show how it links back to what we heard yesterday about Peter's life having been completely changed. When the Holy Spirit touches our lives today he can make big changes. Sing the song together. Today we hear how another man's life was changed competely.

FAST FORWARD
Episode 2 'Bag of Bones' from *On Fire! - The Video*

or

NEWS BROADCAST
(Newsreader sitting inside TV frame.)
Amazing reports are coming in about a disturbance in the Temple. A man was said to be leaping and jumping and shouting 'Praise God!' all over the Temple courts. Local people have told us that this is the same man who has never been able to walk and has spent most of his life begging by the Beautiful Gate. It's all very surprising as the man's recovery appears to have been instant. Reports claim that he was begging in his usual place when two of Jesus' friends met him on their way to the Temple. He asked them for money, but they hadn't got any. Instead these two men, Peter and John, just told him to stand up and walk in the name of Jesus! The man then danced and jumped his way into the Temple. Peter and John said that it happened by the power of the Holy Spirit; it wasn't their power. The authorities in the Temple were not pleased about the healed man. They questioned him, and then the Temple guards arrested Peter and John. We'll keep you informed about these amazing events in Jerusalem.

OVER TO YOU!
Pick up hand, point at children, 'One, two, over to you!'

OFF AIR

OFFICE TIME
5s-6s colour today's film strip.
7s-9s Newsflash sheets.
10s-11s Production Crew Research notes 2.
Hand out 'I've covered it!' stickers.

ON AIR

Boss introduces the Beat the Bong, but before it starts Corrie Scott enters with clipboard and interrupts, 'I demand that my interview is made a priority. I've put hours of work into preparing it!' Boss calms her down. She leaves.

BEAT THE BONG
'How do you feel?' Sam and Terry take three volunteers' names out of the box and the contestants go off-stage to get overalls and blindfolds. Cover the floor and bring on a clear tank filled with a bucket full of cold custard. In the gunge tank sink 10 items – a pencil, an empty cotton reel, a small plastic toy etc. Bring one of the children back. They have a minute to find as many items as possible in the gunge tank. Time this activity with a stopwatch and gong. Keep the score on a large sheet of paper or a blackboard. Volunteers for tomorrow should put names in the box.

STAND AND DELIVER
Draw names from the box to give 'doctor, doctor' jokes.

Boss invites riddles for tomorrow, 'What do you call a ...?' or 'What do you get if you cross a ...?' For example, 'What do you get if you cross a church choir with a pound of minced beef?' A hymnburger!

TAKE 5
Break for drink and biscuit.

ASSIGNMENT 2
THE PRODUCTION CREW

NAME

Now the video needs planning carefully.
Decide what to film and how to put it together.
Talk about it.

Remember - your film should only be ten minutes long.

Tick any of these elements in On Fire! you want to film.

- [ ] BEAT THE BONG
- [ ] INTERVIEWS WITH LEADERS
- [ ] INTERVIEWS WITH CHILDREN
- [ ] KARAOKE PRAISE
- [ ] NEWS BROADCAST
- [ ] SOFA TALK
- [ ] STAND AND DELIVER
- [ ] THE SET
- [ ] INTRODUCTION BY YOUR LINK PERSON
- [ ] SOMETHING ELSE

_____
_____
_____
_____
_____

Day 3
THE RIDDLE

BIBLE MATERIAL: ACTS 8:26-40
INTERVIEW CHARACTER: PHILIP

TODAY'S OBJECTIVES
- To find out how the Holy Spirit guided Philip to explain the scriptures to the Ethiopian official.
- To explore how the Holy Spirit helps us to understand God's word today.

TEAM CHALLENGE
Philip was a deacon in the early church, responsible for the practical aspects of the early church's ministry (Acts 6:1-6), and specifically the distribution of financial aid to those in need. Although his gifts were practical, he spent time listening to God, reading God's word and obeying him. The Ethiopian was of a completely different culture and class to Philip, but was seeking truth. By the Holy Spirit's power, Philip explained Isaiah's prophecy and pointed the man towards faith in Christ.

◆**READ** Acts 8:26-40. God's Spirit had a tremendous effect on Philip. A man the early church recognised for his practical and organisational gifts. Philip listened to the Holy Spirit's prompting and was able to explain the scriptures to the Ethiopian. Even if we see our role as essentially practical, God wants us to listen, understand and respond to him as well. It's not just for those who are called to preach and teach.

◆**READ** Isaiah 53 - the passage the Ethiopian official read. Encourage everyone to share something that God has said to them through this chapter.

◆**PRAY** that today, you will be able to understand and communicate God's truth to the children.

■ YOU WILL NEED:

HEADLINERS
- Photographs of officials, MPs, members of the Royal family.
- Answers to the quiz

POWER PACKS
5s-6s make microphones (see page 62)
- Kitchen foil
- Squares of thin paper (eg computer paper)
- Short lengths of brightly coloured string
- Grey or black dustbin liners cut into squares
- Cardboard tubes
- Small elastic band
- Sticky tape
- Self-adhesive 8mm labels (small round brightly coloured)

7s-9s make flame spinners (see page 62)
- Photocopies, card, two rough-cut spinners for each reporter
- Scissors
- PVA adhesive
- Length of string 90cms long per spinner
- Bradawl (for managers' use only)
- Felt tip pens

BEAT THE BONG: 'WHAT IS IT?'
- Container with children's names in three overalls or old shirts
- Covering for floor
- Small table
- 18 small bowls (six plates to cover the bowls)
- 18 spoons
- six large mixing bowls with cold food in
- Blindfold
- Scoreboard
- Stop watch and gong
- Bucket or bowl
- Sweets or apples for contestants

PROGRAMME AT A GLANCE

	min		min
Registration and Headliners On Fire! song	10	Take 5	5
Fast Forward	5	Sofa Talk	5
Office Time	10	Power Packs	20
Beat the Bong	20	Stand and Deliver	5
	15	Karaoke Praise	15

DON'T FORGET
- Childrens' riddles
- 'I've covered it!' stickers
- Philip in costume, with glasses and Bible.
- Rhoda in costume for appearance at the end of the programme.
- Newspaper billboard with today's headline PHILIP EXPLAINS IT ALL.
- Tomorrow's billboard ready SURPRISE JAILBREAK.

• •

PROGRAMME

REGISTRATION

HEADLINERS
Place the photographs in the headshapes with three alternatives for each person's name and job or title. Managers hand-out Headliner quiz sheets, pencils. Very young children will find this difficult. Managers should be around to give some help. Display answers.

Return clipboards and press passes. Remind children to put riddles in the Stand and Deliver box and names for Beat the Bong.

ON AIR

Boss welcomes children and gives any notices for today.
  Enter Sam: Boss, here's a riddle for you... How many sides has a circle got?
  Boss: I don't know Sam, how many sides has a circle got?
  Sam: Two - one inside and one outside!
  Mention that there will be an opportunity for them to 'Stand and deliver' their own riddles later.
  Empty the Commentary Box. Hand out today's 'post'.

ON FIRE! SONG

'I just don't understand!' This is a light-hearted point in the programme. Boss can say that there are things he doesn't understand. For example, 'I don't understand how they get stripey toothpaste in the tube!' 'I don't understand how my mum always knew when I'd done something wrong just from the look on my face!' 'At school some things were always easy for others, but my teacher spent ages explaining them to me!' Adapt these to suit.

Ask the children what they find difficult to understand, perhaps a subject at school that's just like a riddle to them. Keep this part fast-moving. Interview three or four children. If they don't want to talk, managers, could mention something they find difficult to understand.

FAST FORWARD
Episode 3 'The Riddle' from the *On Fire! - The Video* or

NEWS BROADCAST
(Newsreader sitting inside TV frame.)
  Good evening. Reports are just reaching the newsdesk of a meeting between one of the Jesus group and an official from the Court of the Queen of Ethiopia. The incident took place on the Gaza road, south of Jerusalem. According to reports, the official had been to Jerusalem because he was interested in the Jewish faith. He was reading part of the Bible by the prophet Isaiah when he met Philip, a follower of Jesus. Our Gaza correspondent reports that Philip said, 'God spoke to me through an angel and told me to go to the Gaza road. When I got there, the Holy Spirit prompted me to speak to the man in the carriage.' The foreign official didn't understand what he was reading. Philip explained that the Isaiah was writing about the death of Jesus of Nazareth whose execution we reported recently. This was amazing because Jesus was born hundreds of years after Isaiah's death. Philip told the official that Jesus was the Son of God who had taught the truth about God and healed people. He was killed, but he came back to life just as he said he would. We have received further reports of the Ethiopian man being convinced by this, and being baptised in a stream as a believer in Jesus.

OVER TO YOU!
Pick up hand, point at children, 'One two, over to you!'

OFF AIR

OFFICE TIME
5s-6s colour in today's picture for their film strip.
7s-9s receive Newsflash sheets.
10s-11s use Production Crew Research notes 3.

Play a simple game either in pairs or with the whole group. Give the children a blank piece of paper and a pencil. Clip the paper to the clipboards. Each child keeps his/her paper concealed. Ask them all to think of a TV, cartoon or book character and either write the name or draw the character on the paper. In turn they ask and answer questions giving only a yes/no answer to try to discover each mystery person. The younger ones may need help to ask the right sort of question (eg 'Is your person a man?')

Hand out today's 'I've covered it!' stickers.

ON AIR

BEAT THE BONG
Sam and Terry help draw the names of three contestants for today's game 'What is it?'. Before the children go out to get overalls, explain that today's game involves tasting different foods, so they have the opportunity to change their minds. Assure them that the food will be cold but not 'off' or harmful.

Cover the floor with plastic sheeting. Bring on a small table, a spoon and six cereal bowls. (Replace for each volunteer.) Label mixing bowls with their contents eg cold custard, cold mashed potato, cold pasta, cold tea, cold gravy, cold scrambled egg. Boss shows everyone the contents, and puts a small quantity of each into the bowls. The large mixing bowls should be concealed and the individual bowls covered as the first child is brought onto the stage. He is blindfolded, the covers are removed from the bowls and he has one minute to guess the contents of each bowl. Sam takes charge of the stopwatch and gong. Keep scores as before. Keep a bucket or bowl handy in case the children need to spit out the food! Give contestants a sweet or an apple.

TAKE 5
Break for drink and biscuit.

ON AIR

SOFA TALK 3
Script on page 50.

OVER TO YOU!
Use hand and slogan.

OFF AIR

POWER PACKS
5s-6s make microphones (see page 62) as part of their television equipment and can use for commentaries or interviews with each other.
7s-9s make flame spinners (see page 62)
10s-11s use Production Crew Assignment sheet 3

ON AIR

STAND AND DELIVER
Boss calls up the children who have offered to tell riddles. Sam and Terry could add their riddles eg.

What's green, covered in custard and miserable? Apple grumble!

What's round, red and cheeky? Tomato sauce!

What lies at the bottom of the sea and shakes? A nervous wreck!

What do you call a man with a spade on his head? Doug!

Remind children to put Knock, knock jokes and names in the Stand and Deliver box or give to managers for tomorrow.

KARAOKE PRAISE
Boss recaps on the billboard headlines and stories already covered. Terry brings tomorrow's billboard SURPRISE JAIL BREAK.

OFF AIR

Clipboards and press passes are left with managers. Give children advance notice of the family service or event. (There will be invitations to take home on Day 5.)

■ At the close of today's programme Rhoda should be at the door as the children leave.

NEWSFLASH 3

PHILIP EXPLAINS IT ALL — EXCLUSIVE STORY

Philip must have wondered why the angel sent him to wait by the road and then directed him to talk to the official. Sometimes when we look at things they seen impossible to understand. Philip had the Holy Spirit to help him and before he left him the Ethiopian official did too.

CAN YOU DECODE THIS?

✚ ➡ ■ 〰 ••➤ ☆ ✚ ☆ ⬇

_____

DRAW YOUR NAME IN CODE

_____

_____

God doesn't always want to hide things from us. If you need help to understand something why not ask God to show you? Use this prayer if you want to.

"Dear Father God, I need help to understand why …

_____

_____

Please make it clear to me. In Jesus' name. Amen."

A	♥	J	▢	S	••
B	▲	K	◗	T	⬇
C	■	L	▮	U	🍎
D	✖	M	✓	V	♪
E	✷	N	♠	W	▦
F	○	O	➡	X	⌂
G	◆	P	➤	Y	〰
H	✚	Q	✦	Z	†
I	☆	R	✚		

ASSIGNMENT 3
THE PRODUCTION CREW

NAME

Today you need to make final preparations. Read your job section and carry out the instructions.

CAMERA CREW
Spend time with your director either learning how to use the camera or giving instructions to the camera person and deciding where to shoot from. Write or draw your shooting positions on the storyboard.

INTERVIEWERS
Decide who you will interview and ask their permission.

- ☐ Reporters 5s-6s _____
- ☐ Reporters 7s-9s _____
- ☐ Production Crew _____
- ☐ Managers _____
- ☐ Boss _____
- ☐ Terry/Sam _____
- ☐ Corrie _____
- ☐ Music group _____
- ☐ Others _____

TECHNICAL ASSISTANTS

1 Decide which of you will help the camera people with moving equipment, wires etc. Spend some time with them helping to plan the shots.

2 Find out from the Director if you need any props. Decide which of you will help. Make a big 'The On Fire! Experience' production crew list to be filmed as credits at the beginning or end of your video.

3 Decide who will help to keep the video to ten minutes. Write how many minutes each part of the video should be and add it to the storyboard. Make sure everyone sticks to time when you're filming.

Day 4
ESCAPE!

BIBLE MATERIAL: ACTS 12:1-17
INTERVIEW CHARACTER: RHODA

TODAY'S OBJECTIVES
- To find out about Peter's escape from prison.
- To explore how the Holy Spirit can help us to pray effectively.

TEAM CHALLENGE

There were a large number of Christian believers by now. The authorities were getting worried and Herod Agrippa decided to take action. Persecution began and many arrests were made. James, one of the original twelve disciples, was executed. During the Festival of Unleavened Bread (Exod 12:17; Deut 16:16) Peter was arrested and due to stand trial when the Passover celebrations had ended. Instead of going into hiding, the disciples met to pray. They were certain of the truth of their message and had experienced enough of the Holy Spirit's power to expect God to help them through this situation.

Meanwhile, Peter was involved in yet another miraculous event. God sent an angel to release him from prison. Peter was so surprised, he thought he was dreaming. The prayer group was even more surprised when Peter turned up on the doorstep! They probably thought the knock meant they were about to be arrested; instead it meant their prayers had been answered. Peter was free and their fear turned to joy. Herod Agrippa died soon after (Acts 12:21-23) and God's word continued to spread.

◆**READ** Acts 12 1-17 and reflect on the freedom in this passage. Peter was released from prison, the Passover feast celebrated the Jews' release from Egyptian captivity, the believers prayed and experienced freedom from fear and were released into joy. Is there anything from which you need to be set free today? Pray about these things.

Rhoda was a servant who met with others to pray for Peter's release. Just an ordinary member of the prayer group, she was amazed when her prayers were answered! Rhoda and the others had been praying in the power of the Holy Spirit, they had been praying about a specific situation and they were amazed by the way God chose to answer.

◆**PRAY** together for specific children and about their situations. Look and listen for answers. Expect surprises!

■ YOU WILL NEED

HEADLINERS
- Photographs of famous people known to children - film stars, pop singers, and 'soap' stars. Disguise their appearances by drawing on glasses, a beard or changing hairstyle.
- Answers

PROGRAMME AT A GLANCE

	min
Registration and Headliners	
Flame activity	10
Fast Forward	10
Beat the Bong	10
Power Packs	15
Take 5	20
Stand and Deliver (1)	5
Karaoke Praise	5
Sofa Talk	15
Office Time	5
Stand and deliver (2)	15
	1

BEAT THE BONG: 'RELEASE THE SWEET'
- Nine hard boiled sweets (three green, three red, three yellow)
- Three large shallow bowls containing mashed-up jelly, jam or custard, flour.
- Overalls for children
- Table
- Floor covering

POWER PACKS
- Rigid plastic pots about 90 cm tall to make pencil pots. (Ask pharmacists to save tall plastic tablet containers. These should be washed thoroughly before use.)

- Tissue paper, lace, fabric, sequins, paper strips to cover the pot Photocopies of On Fire! logo reduced in size
- Scissors
- PVA adhesive
- Adhesive sticks

DON'T FORGET
- Small flame shapes for children
- Adhesive stick
- Children's 'knock knock' jokes
- Managers' prepared news items
- 'I've covered it!' stickers
- Rhoda in costume
- Saul and Ananias in costume for appearance at the end of the programme
- Today's billboard SURPRISE JAIL BREAK
- Tomorrow's billboard SAUL HAS CHANGE OF HEART

PROGRAMME

REGISTRATION

HEADLINERS
Managers hand out Headliner quiz sheets, pencils and return clipboards and press passes. Production Crew meet Managers to go through Assignment Sheet 4. They are now ready to start filming today.

ON AIR

Open Commentary Box and distribute post.

Boss points out the large flame and verse on the back of the set and holds up a separate flame with a short prayer written on it. Managers give each of their group members a pencil and a flame. Boss suggests they write or draw a prayer request on it. Stick all flames on backdrop motif. (Emphasise that this isn't a magic formula – God always listens to our prayers.) Invite the children to talk about their prayer flames. Explain that sometimes answers to prayer don't happen immediately; God answers our prayers in many different ways. (Some children may want to share their prayer requests and answers.) Have a few minutes of prayer.

FAST FORWARD
Episode 4 'Escape' from the *On Fire! – The Video*
or

NEWS BROADCAST
(Newsreader sitting inside TV frame.)
The amazing things happening to Jesus' followers have continued. It is all because of the Holy Spirit working in their lives. Today we report that Peter has been arrested and put in prison. This event follows the earlier murder of James, one of the believers, by the command of the king. Many people expected Peter to die in the same way after the Passover celebrations.

Worried friends met to pray about this situation. But there was no hope of escape for Peter because he was chained to his guards and officers were guarding the gate. Reports about Peter in prison say he was calm and relaxed.

The God that these men and women worship doesn't seem to worry about doing the impossible! Apparently he sent an angel into the jail. The angel woke Peter and the chains literally fell off his wrists. The angel told Peter to dress and they both simply walked out of the cell, past the guards and out into the city. Peter hurried to the house where his friends were meeting to pray. A servant girl there called Rhoda was the first person to speak to him after his release. Rhoda just didn't believe that Peter was at the door. When speaking to our reporter, Rhoda said, 'I ran to tell the others that Peter was outside, but no one believed me. Peter kept on knocking and so we finally opened the door to see Peter - at last!'

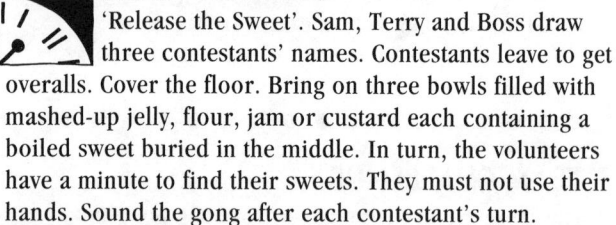

BEAT THE BONG
'Release the Sweet'. Sam, Terry and Boss draw three contestants' names. Contestants leave to get overalls. Cover the floor. Bring on three bowls filled with mashed-up jelly, flour, jam or custard each containing a boiled sweet buried in the middle. In turn, the volunteers have a minute to find their sweets. They must not use their hands. Sound the gong after each contestant's turn.

OVER TO YOU!
Pick up hand, point at children: 'One two, over to you!'

OFF AIR

POWER PACKS
5s-6s and 7s-9s make pencil pots (see page 62).
10s-11s break to use Production Crew Research Notes 4.

TAKE 5
Break for drink and biscuit.

ON AIR

STAND AND DELIVER (PART 1)
Sam and Terry fill in with jokes to keep the session fast moving, eg.

Knock, knock. (Who's there?) Egbert. (Egbert who?) Egbert no bacon!
Knock knock. (Who's there?) Frank. (Frank who?) Frankly, it's none of your business!
Knock, knock. (Who's there?) Howard. (Howard who?) Howard you know without answering the door!

Corrie enters, very cross: I know one!
Knock, knock. (Who's there?)
Corrie. (Corrie who?)

Corrie Scott who's tired of being ignored by everyone. It's got to be time for my interview now!

Boss explains that it's time for Karaoke Praise. She'll have time for her interview later. Corrie storms off.

KARAOKE PRAISE

SOFA TALK 4
Script on page 51.

OVER TO YOU!
Use hand and slogan.

OFF AIR

OFFICE TIME
- 5s-6s complete today's film strip picture.
- 7s-9s Newsflash sheet 4.
- 10s-11s continue filming.

Hand out 'I've covered it!' stickers.

Allow ten minutes of Office Time for the following activity for all groups. Have prayer flames and pencils/pens ready. Each Manager should have prepared a current news item which can be explained simply for the group to think about. It could be about famine or war, or a topic that involves children. Illustrate with news reports, headlines and leaflets from aid agencies. Take care that photographs aren't too horrifying. Spend a few moments together in silence thinking about the needs of these people. Then write prayers on the prayer flames. Collect up all the prayers and explain that whether prayers are spoken out loud or in silence, God hears us. Ask the children to spend a few moments in prayer - out loud or in silence. Explain that it's easier to close our eyes so we don't get distracted. Remind the children before they pray how God miraculously answered Peter's friends' prayers by sending an angel to release him. Managers ask for a volunteer from the group to attach the flame cluster to the large flame shape on the stage later.

ON AIR

One child from each group attaches the prayer flames on the main flame motif. Discuss the prayers as they are added to the backdrop. Sing the On Fire! song as the last flames are being stuck on.

STAND AND DELIVER (PART 2)
At the end of this Rhoda wanders up on to the stage.

BOSS: Rhoda, do you know any knock, knock jokes?
RHODA: Don't talk to me about knock, knock who's there. My friends haven't let me forget what happened the other night!

Exit Rhoda, annoyed.

Tomorrow's billboard SAUL HAS CHANGE OF HEART. Remind everyone about the family service/event. Announce tomorrow's preview of the Production Crew's video 'The On Fire! Experience'. The premiere will be at the family event. Remind contestants and volunteers to hand names in to Managers. Any jokes welcome for tomorrow, or decide on your own topic or type. Children hand clipboards back to Managers.

OFF AIR

■ Saul and Ananias should be seated close the exit doors in deep conversation with their Bibles open.

NEWSFLASH 4

SURPRISE JAILBREAK
EXCLUSIVE

Poor Rhoda! What a shock to hear someone at the door late at night. But imagine the joy and surprise when everyone saw Peter at the house!

How do you think Rhoda felt when she heard the knock at the door? Draw circles around any words you think are true.

FRIGHTENED   HAPPY   SLEEPY

EXCITED   WORRIED   ANGRY

PUZZLED   SAD

How do you think she felt when she saw it was Peter? Draw circles around any words you think are true.

FRIGHTENED   HAPPY   SLEEPY

EXCITED   WORRIED   ANGRY

PUZZLED   SAD

What makes you happy? _____

What makes you sad? _____

But the disciples discovered that nothing is impossible for God.

What do you find impossible? _____

Draw how that makes you feel.

But we can ask God for help with our impossible situations. Fill in and pray this prayer if you want to.

"Dear God, thank you for showing me how you helped Peter by making the impossible happen. This is what I find impossible _____ and I feel _____ Help me with this. In Jesus' name. Amen."

ASSIGNMENT 4
THE PRODUCTION CREW

NAME

Today you're shooting the video!
Check the following things with your Director.
Tick off each one as you go.

☐ ALL THE PRODUCTION CREW ARE HERE.

☐ ALL THE EQUIPMENT, CAMERAS, MICROPHONES AND READY AND WORKING.

☐ INTERVIEWERS HAVE THEIR QUESTIONS READY AND INTERVIEW SUBJECTS ARE HERE TODAY.

☐ LINK PEOPLE HAVE SCRIPTS READY AND HAVE REHEARSED THEIR LINES.

☐ 'THE ON FIRE! EXPERIENCE' PRODUCTION CREW LIST IS READY TO GO ON FILM.

FINALLY!

Listen to the Director as he/she talks you through the storyboard.
Ask if you're not sure about anything.

_____

_____

_____

Day 5
BLINDED

BIBLE MATERIAL: ACTS 9:1-21
INTERVIEW CHARACTERS: SAUL AND ANANIAS

TODAY'S OBJECTIVES
- To find out about the miraculously unexpected events in the lives of Saul and Ananias.
- To explore how exciting it is when the Holy Spirit works in our lives.

TEAM CHALLENGE

Saul's conversion is one of the most dramatic stories in the New Testament and had some of the most far reaching consequences for the early church. Saul was a zealous Jew, who had been a tent-maker before training as a Pharisee in Jerusalem. Saul's father had also been a Pharisee and Saul took his Jewish commitment to the faith very seriously. We first read of him at Stephen's stoning (Acts 7:58) when he looked after the coats of the executors. He had a reputation as a vicious opponent of Christians and even requested permission to track down the Christians in Damascus over 200 km away.

Meanwhile in Damascus, Christians were frightened at the rumours about Saul. Ananias was one of these local Christians. We only read of him on this occasion, although two other people in Acts share his name. God spoke to him in a vision, and quite aware of the possible consequences, Ananias obeyed. He would have had little idea of the far-reaching events that would take place as a result of his obedience. In the meantime, God met Saul on his way to Damascus.

◆**READ** Acts 9:1-21. Ananias' response was 'Here I am, Lord' (10) and he obeyed by going to Saul (17). When God speaks to us we need to obey. This can be hard because of the consequences. Do we worry about the consequences of running a holiday club? What if the children don't come? What if I'm a terrible group leader? What if we mess up the follow-up work? We need to respond as Ananias did and be obedient to God. The rest is the work of the Holy Spirit.

Saul went through a number of dramatic changes. The independent Jewish zealot became a dependent blind Christian. The blind Christian had the scales lifted from his eyes. What an incredible few days! God told Ananias in verse 15, 'Go, because I have chosen him to serve me.' God has 'glorious possibilities' for all our lives and for the lives of the children we have worked with this week.

◆**THANK** God for the 'glorious possibilities' that he has made realities this week for you. Pray that God will work out his 'glorious possibilities' in the lives of the children whom God brings to mind.

■ YOU WILL NEED

HEADLINERS
- Advertisements from magazines and newspapers. Cut off or cover over product name
- Answers sheet

OFFICE TIME
- Thick needle or brooch pin
- Sheet of plain paper
- 'I've covered it!' stickers

BEAT THE BONG: 'BUILD A NEW MAN'
- Two large boxes each containing:
- Pair of trousers (with elastic band, tightly securing the bottom of the trouser legs)
- Old shirt, or jumper (with elastic bands tightly around the wrists and waists)
- Newspapers
- Inflated balloons (two in each box with faces drawn on in permanent marker pens)
- Cardboard tube from a kitchen roll
- Wig

PROGRAMME AT A GLANCE

	min
Registration and Headliners	10
On Fire! song	3
Fast Forward	10
Sofa Talk	5
Stand and Deliver	5
Office Time	20
Take 5	5
Beat the Bong	15
Power Packs	20
'The On Fire! Experience'	10
Karaoke Praise	10
On Fire! song	3

- safety pins
- Sticky tape
- Scissors
- An example man already made
- Stop watch
- Gong

- Sticky tape
- Paper to fit the inside of the lid
- Large pasta shapes, shells, wheels
- Spray paint, yellow, red and orange
- PVA adhesive
- Glue pots and spreaders

- Paul and Ananias in costume.
- Philippian jailer and his wife in costume for appearance at end of programme.
- Today's billboard, SAUL HAS CHANGE OF HEART.
- Write a billboard headline with information about the family service/event for end of programme.

POWER PACKS

5s-6s make a peg clip (see page 63)
- Clothes pegs (one per child)
- Flame shapes for peg clips
- Double-sided sticky tape

7-9s make a pasta collage (see page 63)
- Ice cream/margarine container lids
- Ribbon/tape

DON'T FORGET

- Bin liners containing inflated yellow, red and orange balloons with the verse, 'When the Holy Spirit comes upon you, you will be filled with power'.
- Invitation to the family service/event attached to each balloon. One per child.

PROGRAMME

REGISTRATION

HEADLINERS
Hand out sheets and pencils for children to identify advertisements.

ON AIR

Open Commentary Box. Distribute today's mail.

ON FIRE! SONG
Sing twice. Just as the music finishes, Corrie comes on stage about to throw her usual tantrum, but before she can say anything, Boss tells her that her interview is after Fast Forward (or News Broadcast). Corrie looks taken-aback and says, 'Good!' and storms off.

FAST FORWARD
Episode 5 'Blinded' from the *On Fire! - The Video* or

NEWS BROADCAST
(Broadcaster sitting inside TV frame.)
News has reached us of extraordinary events that took place in Damascus. Saul, who was determined to get rid of the followers of Jesus, and to stamp out their teaching, had an incredible experience. He was thrown to the ground by what appeared to be a powerful flash of lightning. Reports say that Saul heard Jesus speaking to him. The men with Saul were absolutely speechless. Saul was blinded by this experience and was led into Damascus by his men.

Saul insists that he had more messages from God. God said he would send a man who would restore his sight just by laying his hands on him and praying. Further amazing events took place when an elderly man called Ananais claimed that God had spoken to him and told him to go to Saul and to pray for him. Ananais says he trusted God for protection because he knew Saul hated Christians.

Ananias arrived at the house where Saul was staying and spoke to his old enemy calling him 'brother'. He lay his hands on him and the miracle took place. It is claimed that something like fish scales fell from Saul's eyes and he was able to see. When he stood up he was filled with the Holy Spirit which we have heard so much about recently.

SOFA TALK 5
Script on page 51.

STAND AND DELIVER
Invite children to tell their jokes. Terry and Sam on hand with extra jokes.

How many elephants can you get in a mini? Four: two in the front and two in the back!

Waiter, waiter, what's this fly doing in my soup? I expect he's learning to swim!

There were two eggs boiling in a saucepan, one said to the other 'It's hot in here' the other one said 'Just wait, when you get out of here you get your head bashed in!'

OVER TO YOU!
Pick up hand and point at children, 'One two, over to you!'

OFF AIR

OFFICE TIME
- 5s-6s finish their film strip. (If you are holding a family service after the holiday club, colour in and add the sixth picture about the Philippian jailer.) Colour in the end piece.
- 7s-9s Newsflash sheets. Staple the five sheets together to make the newspaper.
- 10s-11s Production Crew Research Notes 5 and finalise arrangements for showing 'The On Fire! Experience'.

Use ten minutes of Office Time for the following activity. Discuss today's topic and listen to the children's understanding of the Holy Spirit. Remind the children that after Saul met with Jesus he couldn't see until Ananias had laid hands on him and prayed.

Each Manager should have pin and paper ready. Whilst discussing the story covered today, stab the pin through the paper making small holes close together in two lines one horizontal and the other vertical to form a cross shape. Practice this beforehand. Continue by saying that today we can receive the Holy Spirit when we come to know Jesus. There was something that Jesus did that was so important that it changes the lives of everyone who believes in Jesus. Ask the children to close their eyes and allow them one at a time to feel the perforated cross-shape. Ask them what the shape is but tell them to wait until everyone has had a turn of feeling the paper before saying anything.

When Jesus died on the cross it was to make it possible for us to go and live with him and Father God one day. Until then we can have his Holy Spirit to help us and make us more like Jesus. Listen to the children's comments and thoughts. Respond to their questions by saying more about Jesus and his death. Don't say too much and risk losing their attention.

Hand out 'I've covered it!' stickers.

TAKE 5
Break for drink and biscuit.

ON AIR

BEAT THE BONG
'Build a new man'. Select eight names to work in two teams of four. Two large boxes should be carried onto the stage (contents listed in 'You will need'). The idea of the game is to build a man by scrunching up the newspaper and stuffing the trousers and jumper with paper. The balloon for the head should be attached to the cardboard tube with tape and pushed into the neck of the jumper. The trousers and top are joined together with the safety pins. Finally the wig goes on top of the balloon. (have an example ready). Give the teams three minutes to build their man and beat the gong at the end of the game.

OVER TO YOU!
Use hand and slogan.

OFF AIR

POWER PACKS
- 5s-6s make peg clips (see page 63)
- 7s-9s and 10s-11s make pasta collages (see page 63)

ON AIR

Boss announces the preview of an important new documentary work 'The On Fire! Experience'. He invites the Production Crew up onto the stage to talk about the video. Applaud as video starts.

Afterwards the Production Crew stand and take a bow. If the video is short and time permits, show the video again.

KARAOKE PRAISE
Boss reminds the children about the family event, pointing out the billboard headline with details. Then Boss draws the children's attention to the flame backdrop and the verse from Acts 1:8 '... when the Holy Spirit comes upon you, you will be filled with power ...'. Ask, 'Have Managers seen the Holy Spirit at work this week?' 'Have Reporters or Production Crew seen him at work?' Listen to answers and spend a short time in prayer thanking God for his Holy Spirit and for all he has done during the week.

ON FIRE! SONG
During the song Terry, Sam, Boss and Managers hand out balloons and invitations to the family event.

Don't forget to give children badges, clipboards, TV sets, plus anything they have made to take home.

OFF AIR

NEWSFLASH 5

SAUL HAS CHANGE OF HEART! **EXCLUSIVE**

Saul knew what he wanted to do. Jesus' friends had to be stopped and he and his men were the people to do it.

Then he met Jesus. The powerful Saul was made weak and blind. He was led to Damascus where God spoke to him again and told him that Ananias would come to him.

But Ananias was frightened to go and see Saul (wouldn't you be?!) But Ananias went and he prayed for Saul. Saul could see again, and received the Holy Spirit.

Pray this prayer if you want to:

"Dear Lord Jesus. I haven't always done the things you would like me to. I'm sorry. Send your Holy Spirit to help me. Amen."

Ananias had to go to Saul. Help him through the maze.

Some people wear glasses to help them see things better. Circle some of the things you would like help to be. I'd like to be

- generous
- good at sports
- kind
- good at school
- a joker
- filled with the Holy Spirit
- rich
- happy
- helpful
- strong
- loving

ASSIGNMENT 5
THE PRODUCTION CREW

NAME

Everyone is going to be shown a preview of the video today. The big showing will be to the rest of the church and your parents at the family service or event.

1. Make sure that the TV and video are working correctly.

2. Write a personal invitation to members of your family or the grownups at home. Make sure you know all the details about the service or event before you fill in the card and cut it out.

An Invitation from the Production Crew

....
is invited to the premiere showing of
THE ON FIRE! EXPERIENCE
at

....

on

....

at

....

From

SOFA TALK 1

Peter is dressed in simple biblical dress. He is confident, calm and uncompromising. Corrie Scott is polite and well-spoken, but begins to get annoyed as the interview fails to go her way.

CORRIE *(to audience)*: Good morning and welcome to our first edition in a new series of Sofa Talk. My name's Corrie Scott and with me today is Peter. As you know Peter has been at the centre of strange events in Jerusalem. I'm delighted he's found time to be with us. *(To Peter)* Good morning, Peter.
PETER: Hello.
CORRIE: I'd like you to tell the viewers of the strange happenings that are reported to have taken place today. I gather that you and other *(glances at sheet and speaks with emphasis)* believers in Jesus of Nazareth, *(looks up again)* had what can only be described as weird experiences.
PETER: It was quite strange, but not as surprising as you may think. Well, Jesus promised to send his Holy Spirit and today he did. That's simply what happened.
CORRIE: Can you confirm that there was a near hurricane rushing through the house and flames were seen leaping from the roof?
PETER *(smiling)*: Well, I think that's a bit over-the-top. Yes, it sounded like a strong wind was in the room and it felt like flames were resting on our heads.
CORRIE: But isn't that all rather strange? I gather that you had the sudden ability to speak other languages.
PETER: Yes, that all came as a bit of a surprise to us. But I've thought about it since and realised that this is exactly what Jesus promised - we simply couldn't imagine what it would be like.
CORRIE: But you talk as if Jesus is still alive. Many of us witnessed his execution less than two months ago. In fact, I was there. I reported on his death. Aren't you simply trying to fool people?
PETER: No not at all. You may have seen him die, but I met him three days later when he came back to life again. He's not dead, hasn't stopped working. It's the Holy Spirit, who is having this effect on us. He gives us the power to do similar things to those Jesus did when he was here.
CORRIE *(more irritated)*: Rushing winds, dead people coming back to life and strange powers. You're only a fisherman aren't you?
PETER: Yes. I was a fisherman until I met Jesus.
CORRIE *(with conviction)*: And is it also true that when this Jesus you speak of with such admiration really needed you - you said that you didn't know him.
PETER: Yes, that's true as well.
CORRIE *(triumphantly)*: So isn't it rather strange that you should be claiming special powers and persuading 3000 more people to join your group today? Many people would say that you're tricking them.
PETER: Well, people are entitled to their opinion. All I know is that once I was a coward who let Jesus down when he was arrested. I was really scared when they killed him and excited when he came back to life. He said I could be his friend again and promised that he would send the Holy Spirit when he returned to heaven. This is what happened today. I suddenly became brave enough to speak the truth and have the power to do it. Yes, I am a simple fisherman. I believe that people decided to follow Jesus because the Holy Spirit worked in them too, not because I was clever. I'm just glad that they were able to hear it in their own languages, wherever they came from.
CORRIE *(crestfallen)*: Er, well, I suppose this is difficult to explain. No doubt we will be hearing more about this as reports come into our news room. I really need to hear more.

SOFA TALK 2

The lame man is dressed in rags and carrying a walking stick or a crutch but not using it. He refuses to sit down (except for one brief moment) and finds it very difficult to stand still. He's in a permanent state of excitement. Corrie Scott is bemused by the story, but she is gradually drawn into the man's enthusiasum.

CORRIE: Good morning and welcome. Today I have with me a man who has never walked until recently. I'm delighted that he's agreed to talk to us.
CORRIE: Er, good morning. Would you like a seat?
MAN: No thanks!! This is the first time I've stood for over forty years, I'm going to enjoy it. (He waves his stick and does a little jump.)
CORRIE: I can see that. Could you tell us what has happened to you?
MAN: Yes!! *(Throws stick/crutch across the stage)* I am better. I feel fine. Today is the first day I have had two legs that walk *(walks across the stage)*, jump *(jumps in the air)*, dance *(a little imitation of tap dancing)* and hold me perfectly steady *(rocks back and forth on his heels)*.
CORRIE: So what exactly happened?
MAN: *(Smiling)*: I got healed.
CORRIE: You mean you saw a doctor who treated you?
MAN: No I do not! I mean healed. I was made well. I got better. Miraculously, supernaturally, amazingly, incredibly, (getting louder) wonderfully, surprisingly, *(very loudly)* praise God!
CORRIE *(Incredulously)*: Are you telling us it just happened?
MAN: Well, yes. I was in my usual place, begging by the Beautiful Gate at the Temple. It was the only way I could survive. I'm over forty years old and I'd never walked until today. Hallelujah! I saw two men I'd

seen before going into the Temple. I asked them for money. They said no, but they'd give me what they could *(beaming smile)*. They gave me legs!!

CORRIE *(Surprised)*: What do you mean?

MAN: I'd never stood up before today *(sits on the very edge of the sofa and leans over confidentially)*. But when Peter told me to stand up in the name of Jesus of Nazareth – I did it!! And my legs have been walking perfectly ever since. *(Walks to the back of sofa and leans on it to demonstrate his walking skills.)*

CORRIE *(Intrigued)*: Is this the Peter we interviewed on a previous programme?

MAN: Yes – and his friend John. Boy, was everyone surprised. Some of these blokes in the Temple have passed me by for years. What a shock they got when I walked in and just enjoyed praising God!

CORRIE *(Laughing)*: I imagine it was a bit of a shock.

MAN *(Walks round to front of the sofa and stands by Corrie)*: Well I was just so excited *(taps her on the shoulder)*. I've calmed down a bit since.

CORRIE *(Relaxed and giggling)*: Really!

MAN *(Walking round the sofa)*: Anyway, I couldn't explain what had happened. Instead, Peter explained about Jesus who was killed here some weeks ago. Well, he came back to life and now those who believe in him have the Holy Spirit who is giving them power to do wonderful things like mend my legs. I don't understand it all. I just know I never walked until today and now, in Jesus' name, I can walk, dance and leap *(demonstrates this)*.

CORRIE: You certainly can! I'm sure we're all very pleased for you, in fact you could say you're a walking miracle! *(She and man laugh at joke)*. Have you anything else you want to say to everyone?

MAN: Yes! *(Shouts while leaping in the air.)* HALLELUJAH!!

SOFA TALK 3

Corrie finds Philip much easier to interview but feels out of her depth when she discovers he's not just a practical man but has experienced the supernatural power of the Holy Spirit. Both seated on the sofa.

CORRIE: Welcome again to this morning's edition of 'Sofa Talk'. I'm delighted to introduce to you one of the men responsible for the distribution of funds among the new religious group who claim that Jesus of Nazareth rose from the dead. Please welcome my guest Philip.

CORRIE: Good morning, Philip.

PHILIP: Good morning.

CORRIE: First of all, can you tell me how you got this job with the Jesus group?

PHILIP: Really because many people are poor. We had already agreed to share absolutely everything we had and distribute it equally. Unfortunately, so many other things were happening that sometimes people felt missed out. So we shared out the jobs. Those who were good at preaching and things would do that and those who were more practically minded would distribute the funds. I just happened to be chosen as one of the seven people who had the job of distributing the funds.

CORRIE: This is interesting. I haven't heard of people who share everything they have before.

PHILIP: We believe it's how Jesus called us to live. It's very important to make sure that everyone has enough.

CORRIE: Yes, I'm sure. Actually it's nice to talk to someone from Jesus group who is practical and isn't making silly claims about strange things happening.

PHILIP: Well, something unusual did happen to me recently.

CORRIE *(Interested)*: Oh yes, what was that?

PHILIP: I was praying when God told me to go down to the old Gaza road. So I went and felt the Holy Spirit tell me to speak to one of the travellers. He was an Ethiopian official on his way from Jerusalem.

CORRIE: Whatever did you say to him?

PHILIP: Well, he'd been to Jerusalem because he'd been interested in God for a long time. He was reading some of Isaiah the prophet. I was able to explain what it meant.

CORRIE *(Surprised)*: You did what? You spoke to a Gentile? Anyway I thought you were a practical man.

PHILIP: Well, I'm not known for my preaching! I'm sure it was the Holy Spirit who helped me to explain it in a way he understood.

CORRIE *(Defensively)*: How do you know he understood?

PHILIP: Because he decided to become a believer.

CORRIE: Now, you seem a very sensible young man. How can you tell this was anything more than coincidence?

PHILIP: I had no reason to be on this road or speak to this man. I was a stranger – why should he believe me? No. I think the Holy Spirit led me there, told me to speak to him and then helped him to believe what I was saying.

CORRIE: Well, thank you for that. It's an intriguing story and we wish you well in your work with the poor.

SOFA TALK 4

Rhoda is dressed in biblical style. She is young and nervous but quite sure about what has taken place. She's not too brilliant at the theory but she is sure of her faith.

Corrie is quite gentle with Rhoda at first, but toughens up when things seem to be out of the ordinary. Both are seated on the sofa. Rhoda is in a quite tense position with her hands clasped and resting on her knees.

CORRIE: Good evening Rhoda.
RHODA *(quietly)*: Good evening.
CORRIE: Rhoda is a servant here in Jerusalem and we've invited her into the studio to tell us about more strange happenings amongst the Jesus followers. Rhoda please tell us a bit about yourself.
RHODA *(quietly)*: Well ... there's not much to tell.
CORRIE: Sorry Rhoda, could you speak up?
RHODA *(louder)*: My name's Rhoda. I'm a servant here in Jerusalem and I believe in Jesus.
CORRIE *(gently)*: I gather after all the recent troubles the authorities have stopped trying to provoke Christians - at least for a while. Tell us about what happened.
RHODA: It was all really scary. Lots of Jesus' followers had been taken away and James had been killed. Then Peter, who was one of the main leaders, got arrested. He was really brave, but the rest of us were dead frightened.
CORRIE *(with understanding)*: It must have been awful. What did you do?
RHODA: We went to a safe place and prayed.
CORRIE: Prayed? Wouldn't it have been better to organise a protest, appeal to the public, you know, do something?
RHODA *(with more confidence)*: I don't know. Praying seemed like the best thing - and in fact it was.
CORRIE: Why do you say that?
RHODA: Because it worked! *(getting excited)* Peter was in prison, so we met to pray for him. As we were praying there was a knock on the door. It was my job to answer it and I was so surprised to hear Peter's voice at the door that I forgot to open it! It took me ages to persuade the others that it was Peter and that we should let him in.
CORRIE: So how did he escape? *(confidentially)* Tell me which one of you helped him.
RHODA: It wasn't one of us. It was God. He sent an angel to let Peter out.
CORRIE *(amazed)*: Do you really believe that?
RHODA *(confidently)*: Yes. Of course I do!
CORRIE: That's amazing! But maybe it was one of your friends who got Peter out?
RHODA: Then why didn't anyone see Peter go? He was chained to two guards and he just got up and walked out of the prison. If there had been someone helping they would have been seen.
CORRIE *(grudgingly)*: Well, perhaps. But what do you think happened?
RHODA: God did it all. We prayed and he answered. I don't think we had quite expected it to be like that. But it doesn't matter. We were just pleased to see Peter again.
CORRIE: Thank you Rhoda for coming on the show today. It's yet another unusual story to come from the Jesus group.

SOFA TALK 5

Saul is dressed in smart biblical-style dress. He's confident and quite brash, but has changed from being a bully. He has quite a cultured accent. Ananias is dressed in plainer biblical style. A trustworthy self-effacing older man. He has a country accent. Corrie expects a fight between two opposing sides.

CORRIE: Good evening gentlemen.
SAUL: Good evening.
ANANIAS: Good evening.
CORRIE: We have quite a programme for you today - a real exclusive. Here on the same sofa is a follower of Jesus from Damascus. His name is Ananias. Next to him is Saul, a well-known figure in Jerusalem well known for persecuting followers of Jesus. So, Saul, can you tell us why you are prepared to share a sofa with Ananias. Unless of course you are plotting to have him arrested after this programme, ha ha!
SAUL: Well, I'm not interested in getting at Jesus' followers anymore - in fact I've joined them! Ananias is a good friend.
CORRIE *(rather deflated - shuffling her notes and trying to recover)*: Hmm, perhaps we can move on to you Ananias. Aren't you scared about sitting here with Saul?
ANANIAS: No, absolutely not! I would have been terrified a few weeks ago. In fact I was a bit scared the first time I met him.
CORRIE: Why? Tell us about it.
ANANIAS *(slowly and deliberately)*: Well, I'd heard a rumour - that Saul had arrived in Damascus in order to sort out the followers of Jesus. So naturally, I began to pray about it. While I was praying, God spoke to me. He told me to go to a particular house in Damascus.
CORRIE: You're joking.
ANANIAS: No. God always knows what

he's talking about. Anyway I went even though my knees were knocking, I can tell you. When I met him I didn't need to be scared at all, and he was blind. So, with the power of the Holy Spirit I put my hands on him prayed and he could see again.

CORRIE: Wasn't that a bit dangerous?

ANANIAS *(thoughtfully)*: I suppose so. But God told me not to worry, and it was all fine in the end because I discovered he'd met Jesus.

CORRIE *(triumphantly)*: Ah ha! Now even if you say you believe that Jesus rose from the dead, he's not still here on earth, so how could you have met him Saul - er Paul?

SAUL: On my way to Damascus something strange happened. I was totally determined to get at these people who believed in Jesus. But before I got there a flash of lightning came from the sky and I fell to the ground. When I came to, there was Jesus, speaking to me. It was quite amazing When it was all over, I found I was blind - I was taken into Damascus and you know the rest.

CORRIE: This is incredible, but why should anyone believe you?

SAUL: No one has to if they don't want to. But I do have witnesses. I had several companions who heard the voice also. Why else would I be sitting here with Ananias if it wasn't true?

CORRIE *(slightly flustered)*: Well, we've heard a number of strange stories from the Jesus group recently. We've just got a few minutes. Paul do you want to say anything to the viewers at home?

SAUL: Yes. I was blind, now I can see. I hated believers in Jesus now I am one. Believing in Jesus has totally changed me and the power of the Holy Spirit helps me to do all kinds of things for God. If God can do this for me, he can do it for you.

SOFA TALK 6

Philippian jailer in Roman-style dress holding a large bunch of keys. He is honest and quietly spoken. Jailer's wife is also in Roman-style dress. An ordinary but excitable lady who has enjoyed the drama of it all. Three children are invited to stand round or sit on the edge of the sofa throughout.

CORRIE: Hello everyone. This is the first of a new series of regular features on 'Sofa Talk' called 'Meet the Family'. Every week we will be meeting an ordinary family who will tell us about an extraordinary event in their lives. Today our guests are a prison officer and his family from Philippi. *(Smiling and turning to them)* Hello everyone.

EVERYONE: Hello.

CORRIE: It's good to meet you, your wife and your three lovely children. First of all can you tell us about your job?

JAILER: It's quite simple really. Criminals are brought to the prison and chained in a cell. They've usually been beaten up as well, so it's not too difficult to keep them there. I just feed them and make sure they're safe.

CORRIE: So every day's pretty much the same for you; nothing too unusual happens.

JAILER: Well no – not until last week.

CORRIE: What happened?

JAILER: It was all a bit strange from the start. We had two Jewish blokes brought in. I chained them and left but after a while I heard singing.

CORRIE: Singing?

JAILER'S WIFE: Singing! Is that what you call it? You could hear them down in the market square.

CORRIE *(confused)*: Sorry, but I'm not following. Why were they singing?

JAILER: They weren't really criminals – they'd been brought in on a religious charge. They were two of the new Jesus people and they have a reputation for praising God a lot.

CORRIE: They couldn't be put in prison for that, surely?

JAILER: Oh no it wasn't that. They'd upset some of the locals by getting rid of an evil spirit from the local fortune teller. It meant she couldn't make any more money.

JAILER'S WIFE: What a do that was! She'd been following these two blokes for days - shouting and screaming. Then they rid her of the spirit and fights broke out everywhere ...

CORRIE *(interrupting)* ... er thank you. Can we get back to the story? I suppose if this involves Jesus' friends you're going to tell me something miraculous happened?

JAILER: Well yes. Eventually the singing got louder and then there was a rumbling noise - in fact it was an earthquake! The prison shook and then it began to fall round my ears.

CORRIE *(triumphantly)*: Ah, an earthquake! I can explain that!

JAILER: That's not the whole story! The miracle as far as I'm concerned is that no one escaped.

CORRIE: What, no one?

JAILER'S WIFE: No - and a good thing it was too. They'd have had his guts for garters *(points at her husband)*. In fact, he was ready to top himself until he realised they were all there!

CORRIE: So what happened next?

JAILER: It gave me the shakes I can tell you! I was so impressed with Paul and Silas and their singing and what God had done for them, I asked them what I could do to be saved.

CORRIE: And what did they say?

JAILER: They told me to believe in Jesus and now I do. What a difference it's made to me!

JAILER'S WIFE: I'll say. He brought these two chaps home in the middle of the night - in the middle of an earthquake!

CORRIE *(interrupting)*: Quite. So how did that make you feel - having to provide for all these midnight visitors?

JAILER'S WIFE: Oh, it was marvellous. Well, apart from all the excitement, it was wonderful to hear about Jesus. Me and the children were just as excited as my husband. We all got baptised straight away *(laughing)*. In the middle of the night. It gave the neighbours something to talk about.

CORRIE: Thank you. One final question. What was the most exciting part of that eventful evening?

JAILER: Oh that's easy. Getting to know Jesus. Exciting events come to an end, but the difference he's made to our family is permanent.

ALL-AGE SERVICE

An all-age service or event is an ideal opportunity to invite the families and friends to see what the children have been doing at On Fire! It will give a taste of the activities and can form part of a church's evangelistic strategy among families. The set, managers, and office teams should be as they have been throughout On Fire!

SETTING
Set up the church using some of the On Fire! set items and the large flame motif.

The music group play the tune to the On Fire! song as the congregation arrives. Everyone is handed a link of a paperchain with double-sided sticky tape attached to one side, and a pen and sit with their children's manager.

WELCOME AND HYMN
The leader should greet the congregation and help them to feel at home in the studio or church.

Open with a well-known hymn likely to be familiar to visitors. In an opening prayer commit your time to God and ask him to send his Holy Spirit to speak today.

PRAYER
A manager and a child from each group of Reporters and Production Crew say a prayer. Include a range of prayers:
- thanking God for what has happened during On Fire!
- asking for his Holy Spirit to keep working in our lives at school and at home
- praising him for his love and desire to change us.

BIBLE READING
Acts 16:16–40

FAST FORWARD
Show 'Midnight Dungeon' from *On Fire! – the Video* or

NEWS BROADCAST
(Newscaster sitting inside TV frame.)

"Good morning. Here is the news.

Reports of the empowering of the Holy Spirit and the miraculous events surrounding the followers of Jesus of Nazareth continue to reach us.

Again we have news of Paul, whose life was changed completely when he met Jesus and became a believer. He once preached persecution and now speaks of the love of Jesus and forgiveness of sins for everyone. We hear today that Paul and his companion Silas were pestered by a slave girl with an evil spirit. They actually ordered it out of her in the name of Jesus. The evil spirit helped the girl to tell people's fortunes. Her owners were so angry because of loss of earnings that they insisted that Paul and Silas be severely beaten and thrown into jail. We have heard before of how the disciples of Jesus weren't put off by desperate crises. Instead of being fearful about their future, these men sang praises to their God and spoke to other prisoners about Jesus!

Our correspondent in Philippi said that at midnight a massive earthquake occurred with the jail in the direct line of the quake. The doors were flung open and all chains and securing devices were broken.

The jailer was convinced that the inmates had fled during the quake. The Philippi Prison Authority can insist on a death warrant for prison staff who fail to take adequate security measures. Friends say that he believed suicide was the only option. Our correspondent says that the prisoners actually remained in the prison and Paul and Silas actively encouraged the jailer against suicide. So amazed at their courage and honesty, the jailer fell at Paul and Silas' feet trembling. He wanted to know how he too could become a follower of Jesus. Paul and Silas explained he had to believe in the Lord Jesus they then told him more of who Jesus is and what he came to do. The jailer took Paul and Silas (his prisoners) to his own home and introduced them to his wife and children. They too became believers and were filled with joy because they now belonged to God's family."

SOFA TALK
(Script on page 52)

The sofa talk involves the Philippian jailer and his family. Ask three children to join them on the sofa as part of the family. Choose one from each On Fire! age group.

KARAOKE PRAISE
Sing some of the children's favourite songs from On Fire! Boss could wander around with the microphone to both the children and adults who he/she knows will be willing.

PRAYER CHAINS

Point out that the flames in the set represent prayers that the children have prayed. Say if any of the prayers have been answered. Explain the prayer chain activity. Each person thinks of something that they want to talk to God about. The prayer chain is both a reminder of the story about Paul and Silas released from prison and a sign that we are joining together in prayer. Invite people to write or draw their prayer on their chain link and attach it to the link of the person next to them. Managers collect the chains from the end of their rows and attach them to the edges of the flame motif on the set so that the chains flow away from the flame.

OFFICE TIME

Members of the Production Crew say a few words about what they have done. Show the video of 'The On Fire! Experience'. Managers from the Reporters show a TV set with finished film and finished newspaper. The Leader could say 'Over to you!' pointing at Boss and other key team members. Invite them to the front for short interview. What have they learned from On Fire!? How has *their* faith grown through thinking about the Holy Spirit?

ON FIRE! SONG

Sing the theme song for the last time. Invite people to ask God to help them experience the work of the Holy Spirit in a new way or perhaps for the first time, so that the words of the song become real to them.

ALL-AGE EVENT

If the children's families and friends would not be at home in a church building, it may be a good idea to hold a barbeque, sports day or barn dance. Make sure everyone feels welcome. Elements of On Fire! could be included in a more informal way. Choose some Beat the Bong games and craft activities. Set up each activity as a stall run by the children with the help of their managers. Give families and friends thirty minutes to try out some. Include the paper chain activity, the final episode of *On Fire! - The Video* and, of course, 'The On Fire! Experience'.

You might want to advertise the event as 'all-age' rather than 'family' if single people or lone parents are likely to understand 'family' only as nuclear family.

Day 1 ALIGHT!

The Production Crew Research Notes

NAME _____

BIBLE BASE: (NEW TESTAMENT) ACTS 2:1-41
INTERVIEW SUBJECT: PETER

BACKGROUND INFORMATION

Why were the disciples meeting behind locked doors?

_____

What or who changed Peter?

_____

How did the crowd react to this change in Peter?

_____

What other questions would you want to ask Peter?

Day 2 BAG OF BONES

THE PRODUCTION CREW Research Notes

NAME _____

BIBLE BASE: ACTS 3:1-10
INTERVIEW SUBJECT: THE LAME MAN

BACKGROUND INFORMATION

What was so amazing about this man being healed?

_____

Peter and John called upon someone to heal the man. Who was it?

_____

What were the lame man's reactions?

_____

Have you seen God's Holy Spirit at work in people's lives? In your own? What happened? Who led him out of prison?

Day 3 THE RIDDLE

THE PRODUCTION CREW Research Notes

NAME _____

BIBLE BASE: ACTS 8:26-40
INTERVIEW SUBJECT: PHILIP

BACKGROUND INFORMATION

How did Philip know where to go?

_____

Who did he meet?

_____

What was he asked to do?

_____

What questions would you want to ask Philip about the Bible?

Day 4 ESCAPE

THE PRODUCTION CREW Research Notes

NAME _____

BIBLE BASE: ACTS 12:1-17
INTERVIEW SUBJECT: RHODA

BACKGROUND INFORMATION

How was Peter released from prison?

_____

Who led him out of prison?

_____

What was Rhoda's first reaction to Peter's arrival at the prayer meeting?

_____

Rhoda didn't believe her ears. How would you react to something that seems impossible?

_____

Day 5 BLINDED

THE PRODUCTION CREW Research Notes

NAME _____

BIBLE BASE: ACTS 9:1-21
INTERVIEW SUBJECTS: SAUL AND ANANIAS

BACKGROUND INFORMATION

What sort of person was Saul before he met Jesus?

_____

Ananias knew he had to see Saul. What does this tell us about Ananias?

_____

When Ananias prayed, Saul was able to see again. What else did Saul 'see'?

_____

Ananias called Saul 'brother' because they were both members of whose family?

예수님이 FIRE다

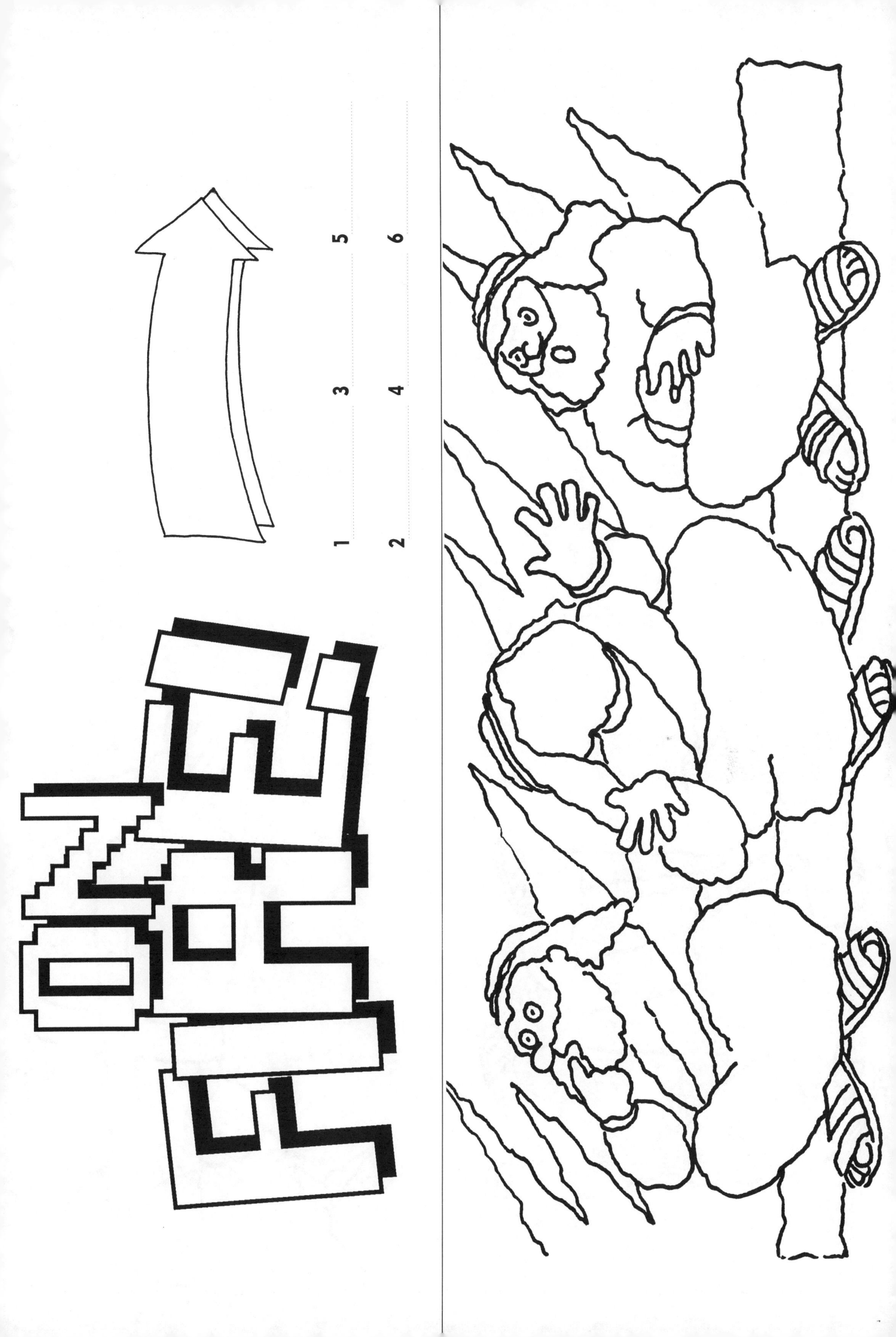

↑

1   3   5
2   4   6

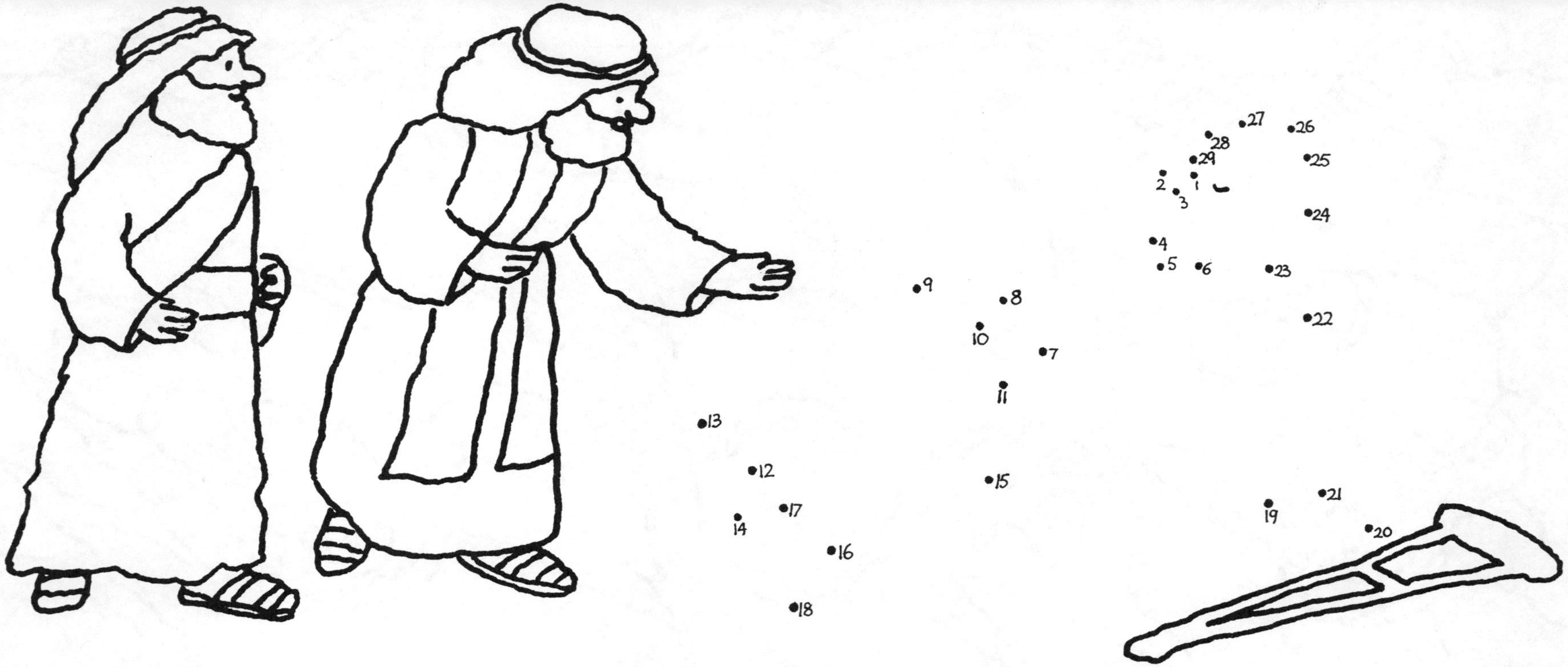

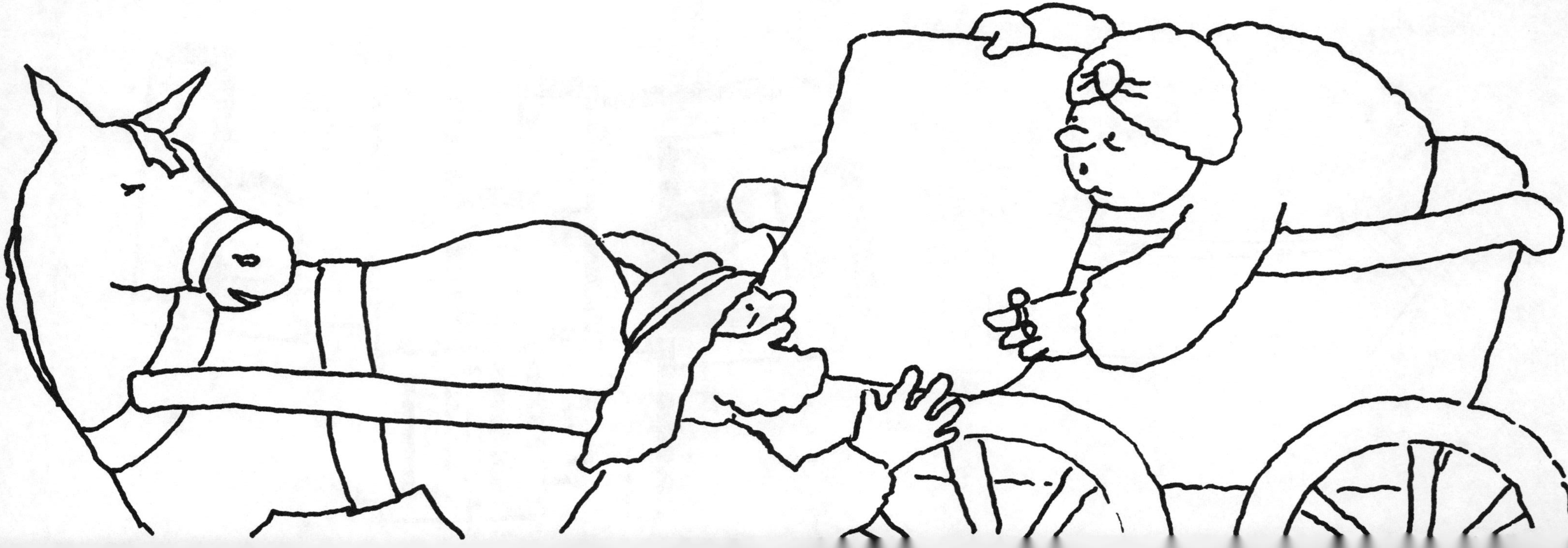

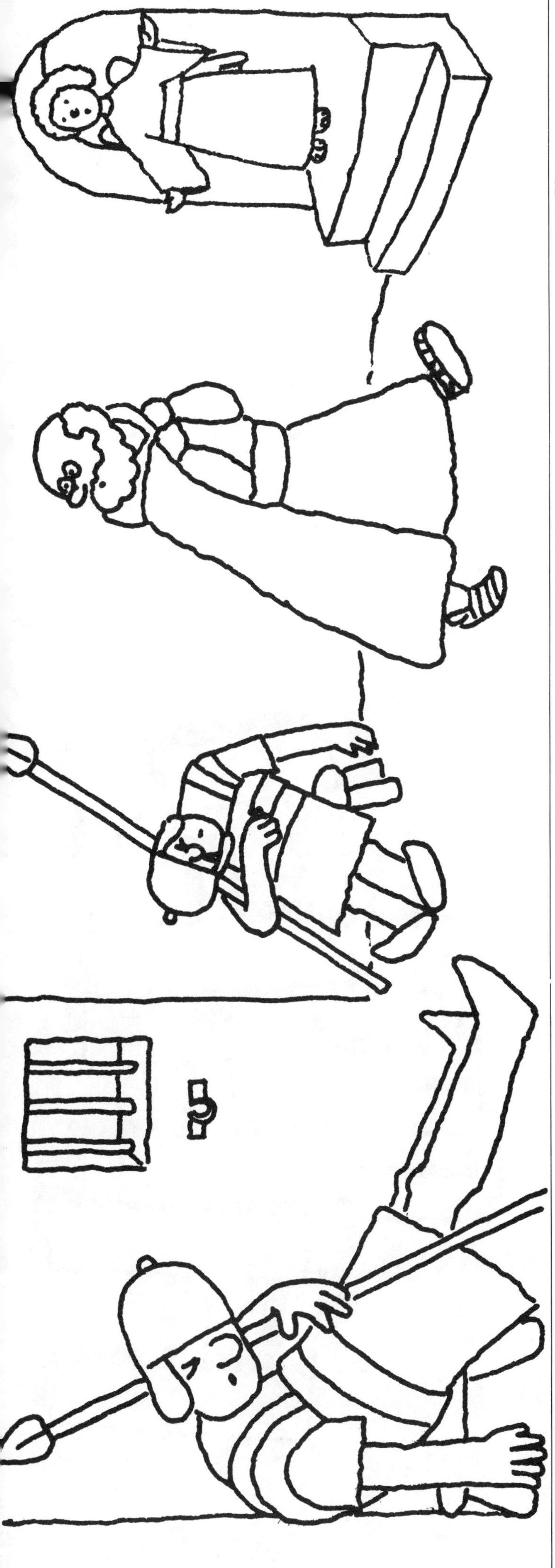

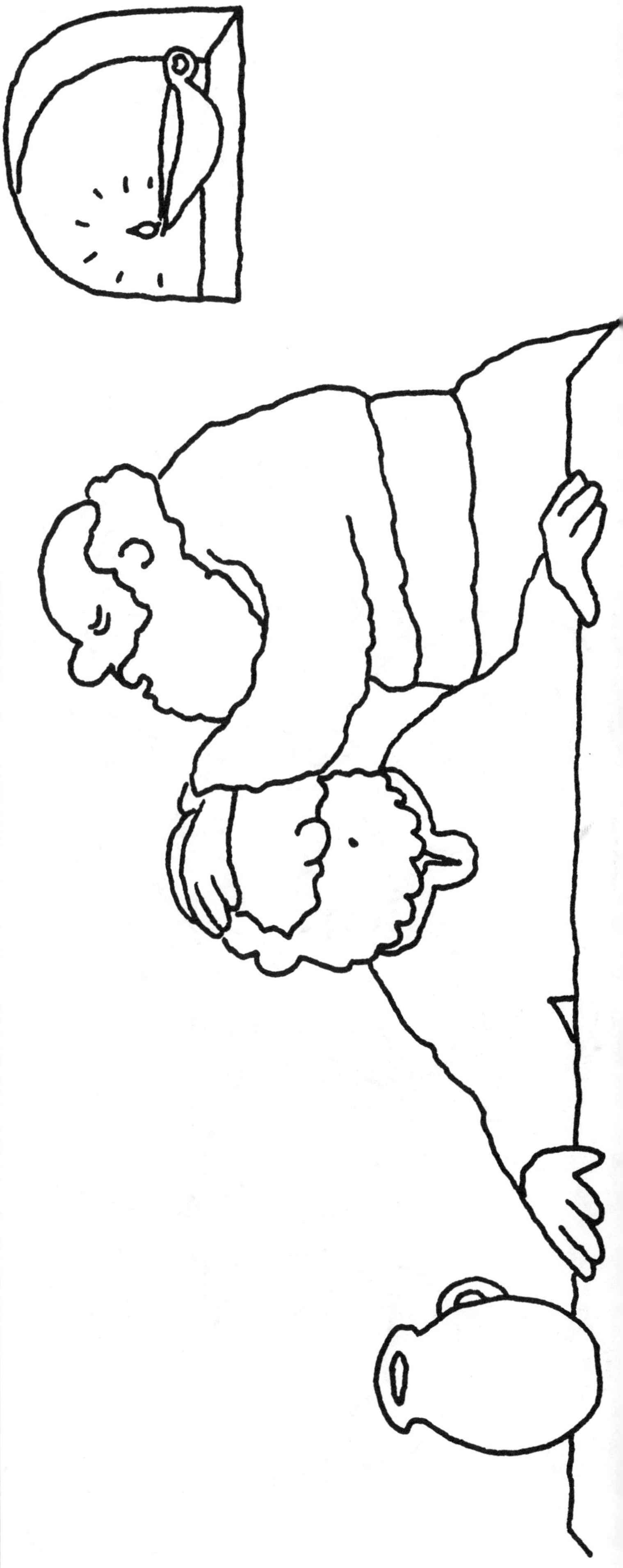

ON FIRE!

REPORTED BY _____

CLIPBOARDS (Day 1)
- Strong A4 card
- Bulldog clips (one per board)
- Collage materials (paper, tissue paper, flame shapes)
- PVA adhesive and spreaders
- Photocopies of logo
- Pictures fom magazines
- Scissors
- White stickers

Cover the card with plain paper. Allow the children to create their own designs with the collage materials. Label with the child's name.

TV SETS (Day 2)
- Shoebox (1 per child)
- Squash bottle tops or tube tops for knobs
- PVA adhesive
- Paper to cover boxes
- Sticky tape

Cut slits on front of box 10 cm long, 23 cm apart. Reinforce slits with sticky tape. Children cover shoeboxes with paper and stick on knobs. Ensure all TV sets are labelled with the child's name.

PAPER FASTENER MEN (Day 2)
- Paper fasteners (seven per child)
- Felt tip pens/crayons
- Scissors
- String (optional)
- Bradawl or holepunch- to make holes for paper fasteners (for leaders' use only.)

Photocopy 'man' from page 64 onto card. Older children can cut out their own, younger ones will need help. Colour him in and fit on his head, arms, legs with paper fasteners. If you wish, punch a small hole at the top of his head and ends of limbs, attach threads to the four points marked X

61

MICROPHONES (Day 3)
- Small cardboard tubes
- Kitchen foil (cut into strips, sufficient to cover the tube)
- Kitchen foil (cut into squares)
- Grey bin liners (cut into squares)
- Thin paper to scrunch-up (computer paper is ideal)
- Self adhesive shapes (8mm round, brightly coloured)
- Short lengths of coloured string
- Sticky tape
- Small elastic bands

Wrap the square of foil round the ball-shaped computer paper – leave a 'tail' on the foil to fit in the tube. Cover the 'microphone head' with the square of bin liner and secure at bottom with a small elastic band. Wrap foil around cardboard tube. Stick the microphone head into the tube and attach the self adhesive labels onto the tube. The 'microphone wire' string should be stuck in the bottom of the tube.

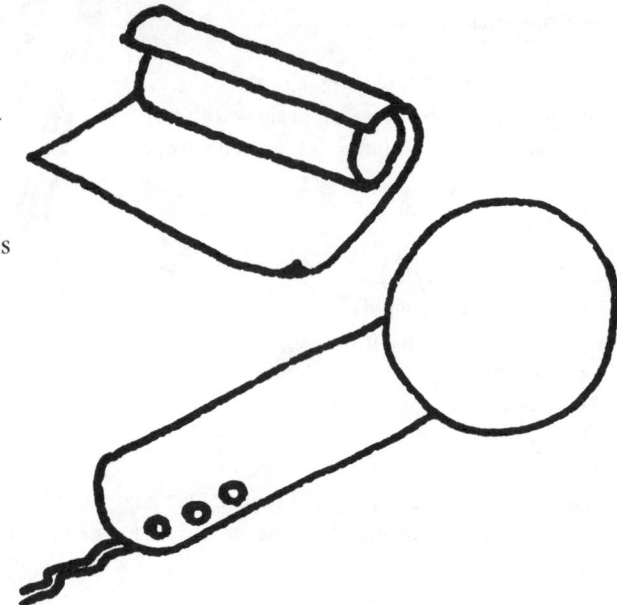

FLAME SPINNERS (Day 3)
- Spinner design from page 64 photocopied and stuck onto card
- Thin string approx 90cm long
- Sharp-point to make holes for string (For leaders' use only)
- Felt tips
- PVA adhesive
- Scissors

Cut out the spinners roughly, stick the two circles together then finish cutting the edges. Colour in the flame shapes, using red, yellow and orange. (Leaders should make the holes in the spinners.) Insert the string and knot the ends of the looped string together. Place the looped string over the forefinger on each hand, twist the spinner round but holding one hand still and making circle movements with the other, twisting the string. Gently pull hands apart and relax slightly.

PENCIL POTS (Day 4)
- Washed tablet containers (ask local chemists to save them for you)
- Strips of sugar paper or fabrics
- Collage materials and paper shapes/flames
- Photocopies of On Fire! logo, or lace, sequins etc. if using fabrics
- PVA adhesive and spreaders
- Scissors

Children cover and design their own pencil pots using craft materials as they wish.

PEG CLIPS (Day 5)
- Clothes pegs
- Double-sided adhesive
- Felt tips or fluorescent crayons
- Scissors

Draw or photocopy flame shapes from page 13 or page 64 onto card. Older children will be able to cut their own. The younger ones should have theirs prepared for them. Colour the flames. Stick the double sided adhesive to the peg and attach to the underside of the flames.

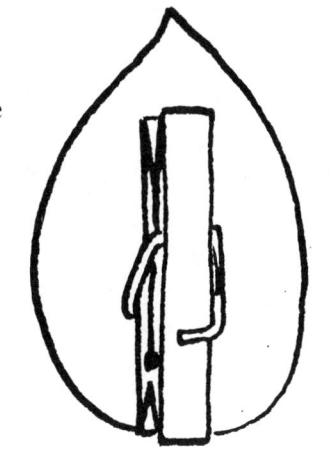

PASTA COLLAGE (Day 5)
- Large pasta shapes (shells/bows/wheels)
- Spray paints in red/orange/yellow. (For leaders' use only.)
- Ice cream tub lids, large margarine tub lids
- Coloured paper (pre-cut to fit inner rim of the lid to make a frame)
- PVA adhesive and spreaders
- Loops of ribbon/tape for hanging the collage
- Sticky tape

Spray pasta in advance and have a selection of shapes and colours available for the children to choose from. The coloured paper should be stuck as backing paper in the lids. The children can then make their own designs with the pasta sticking them with PVA adhesive. Add the loop with sticky tape to the back of the finished pasta collage.

■ EXTRA CRAFT ACTIVITIES

INITIAL STAMPS
- Tracing paper and pencils
- Inked stamp pads
- Light string (not plastic)
- Small wooden blocks (unvarnished)
- Scissors
- PVA adhesive and spreaders or double-sided tape

Help each child to write their initials onto a piece of tracing paper slightly smaller than the blocks of wood. Turn the tracing paper over and go over the pencil letters imprinting the initials onto the wood (the initials will be written backwards). Stick the string along the pencil lines. When dry, press onto the ink pad and print initials.
*This activity is suitable for older children.

WIND STREAMERS
- Long roll of crepe paper
- Thin garden stakes
- Double-sided sticky tape
- Scissors

Cut folded or rolled crepe paper in strips 7 cm apart (this will produce long streamers 7 cm wide). Attach the paper streamers to the stakes with tape. Streamers blow in the wind outside making patterns, or inside by making circular arm movements.

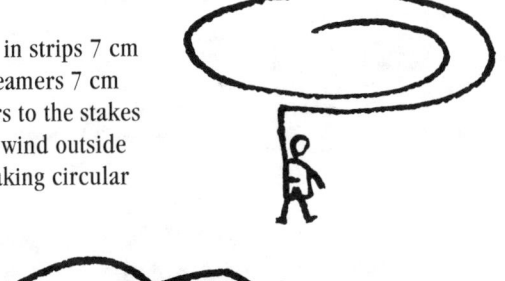

PAPER FASTENER MEN (Instructions on page 61)

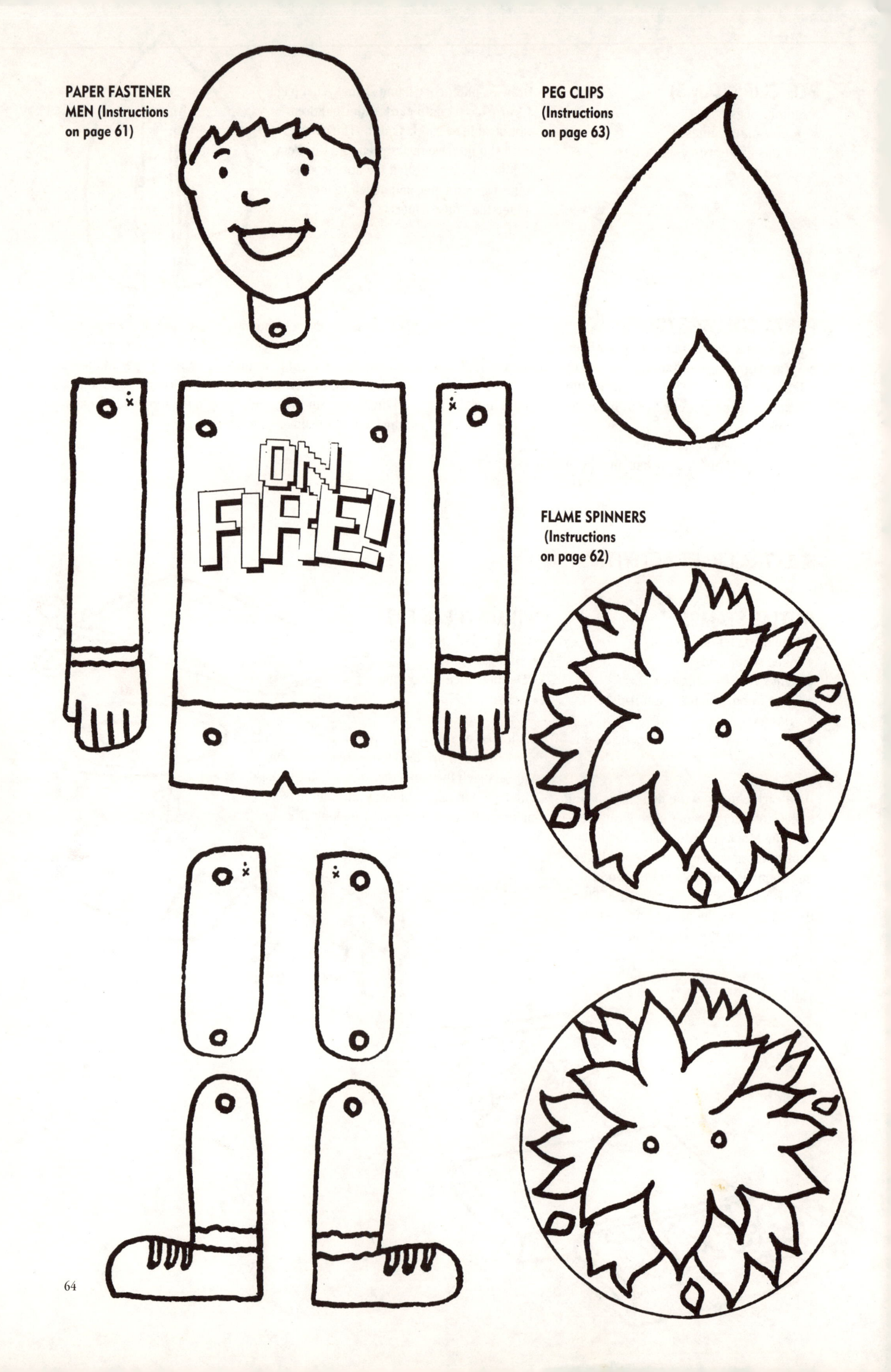

PEG CLIPS (Instructions on page 63)

FLAME SPINNERS (Instructions on page 62)

ON FIRE!